UNWIRED
Awaken What AI Can't Replace

The Human Code to Consciousness, Creativity
& Capital in the Age of Acceleration

TARUN KISHNANI

Published by:

OWL®
PUBLISHERS

www.owlpublishers.com
360 S Market St, San Jose, CA 95113,
United States.

Printed in the United States of America

WHY AWAKEN THE INTELLIGENCE THAT IS INNATE WITHIN US?

Everywhere I go, I hear the exact alarming prediction: "Humans are losing their jobs." Headlines announce massive job losses, shorter workweeks, and suggest that soon humans might not even need to work at all. AI-powered robots, we are told, already handle over half of the tasks traditionally performed by humans at home and in the workplace. Experts—from the world's richest leaders to consulting giants, the World Economic Forum, and even multilateral institutions like the World Bank, International Monetary Fund—warn that in just five to seven years, we could lose more than 500 million jobs globally. And these, they say, are conservative estimates.

But what if I told you that this is fear-mongering at its finest?

The reason I wrote this book is rooted in a question I've heard repeatedly from experts and everyday people alike:

"Will AI take my job?"

My simple, confident answer is NO.

This book exists because within each of us lies an innate intelligence— something uniquely human, irreplaceable by any machine or algorithm. AI might perform tasks faster, but it cannot dream, create deeply meaningful connections, or cultivate genuine emotional intelligence. AI can replace tasks, not humans.

This innate human intelligence, awakened consciously, empowers us not only to survive but to thrive in an AI-driven world.

This book is your guide to awakening and harnessing that power.

PURPOSE

If I'm sincere, I first wrote this Human Code for myself. It began as scattered diaries filled with notes, ideas, and reflections gathered everywhere—at business conferences, lunches, meetings, dates, spiritual retreats, yoga studios, Zoom calls, and even during simple daily moments like reading in my library, showers, or spontaneous conversations. Capturing these thoughts was challenging; many powerful epiphanies arose to me when I had no way to record them, yet they somehow returned when I needed them most.

Assembling these fragmented insights into a single manuscript became my own journey toward clarity and deeper understanding. Reading the completed manuscript, I was struck by how clearly these dictums, practices, and thoughts had elevated my own life, consciousness, creativity, and critical thinking. I realized this collection wasn't just for me; perhaps it was always meant for you, too.

This isn't a guide on how to become more successful or enlightened; it's simply an invitation, from my heart to yours, to pause, slow down, and reconnect with the wisdom already within you. AI can automate almost anything, but it cannot replicate your quiet inner voice that dreams, feels deeply, and creates meaning.

As you read, gently pause, breathe deeply, and ask yourself just one question:

"What do I genuinely wish to create with this precious life?"

✹ NOTE TO THE READER

This book is not just a collection of ideas to ponder—it's an invitation to experience.
Every concept you'll read here has been lived, practiced, and tested by me. The methods are simple—sometimes so simple that they're easy to overlook—but their power lies in their simplicity.

You'll find practices drawn from both ancient wisdom and modern neuroscience: breathing techniques to calm the mind, mindful rituals to reset your energy, and creative prompts that rekindle focus and flow. These are not theories; they are tools I've personally used to clear mental noise, reconnect with stillness, and create real inner growth.

You'll also come across checks on yourself throughout the chapters. Consider these as pauses—a moment to look inward, to integrate what you've read, and to feel the subtle shift that happens when awareness deepens.

I created that to enhance my own productivity and regain my energy.

I now humbly offer you the opportunity to experience this for yourself.

The goal is not more noise, but clarity: to help you reconnect with your inner awareness, and to awaken in you what AI can never replace.

With the Blessings of the Divine and My Dear Shree Ganeshaya Namah – The destroyer of evils, obstacles, and most importantly the bestower of Harmony, Peace, and Wisdom…

Om Gam Ganpathiye Namah!

Contents

"Energy cannot be created or destroyed; it can only be changed from one form to another." — Albert Einstein.

CHAPTER 1: ENERGY

The Frequency AI Can't Replicate

"Before thought, before breath, there was vibration.

That is, you."

You Are Energy: Your Original Operating System

Take a deep breath. Close your eyes. Now, gently open them after counting to three.

Even in the chaos of your day, right here, right now.

Sense that gentle vibration, the subtle hum under your skin. It's soft, initially barely perceptible, like a whisper of life. This rhythm existed well before your first heartbeat, breath, or thought. It represents your most natural state—wireless, securely encrypted, unhackable, and seamlessly alive.

This is more than just poetry. It's your unique internal operating system, a quiet symphony guiding you from inside, a pure intelligence that never crashes, never needs updates, and cannot be hacked. It is completely Unwired.

The Silent Symphony inside You

It merely exists. When life becomes overwhelming or when a sense of disconnection arises, return to this subtle vibration. This resonance beneath your ribs transcends merely being your heartbeat; it serves as your direct connection to something ancient, eternal, and profoundly human.

Take a deep breath now. Feel this truth clearly:

You are more than just a drop in the ocean; you embody the entire ocean vibrating within a single drop.

One Breath Closer to the Truth

Every time you inhale, you become one breath closer to the most actual reality of this material form — death.
Not as fear.
Not as a tragedy.
But as clarity.

This life — your relationships, your ambitions, your fears, your stories — is fleeting by design.

Everything around you is temporary, and that is precisely what makes it precious.

Everything Is Energy and Has Always Been That Way

Not long ago, scientists thought the universe was made of solid, unmoving objects—atoms fixed firmly in place. Today, physics shows something even more astonishing:

Everything in your surroundings is energy vibrating at various frequencies.

You, me, the chair you're sitting on, and the sunlight streaming through your window—all of it vibrates. Atoms spin and whirl, electrons pulse, and nothing remains completely still. The universe, from galaxies to the cells in your fingertips, is a symphony of frequencies.

Modern research shows that the human body resonates at specific, measurable frequencies. Standing, your body vibrates at approximately 7–8 cycles per second (Hz), while sitting, it's around 4–6 Hz. Each organ—heart, brain, and others—produces its distinct note in this intricate harmony. Every cell emits tiny electromagnetic signals, creating an invisible, continuous musical background that persists throughout your life.

But how could ancient civilizations have known this long before modern science? Thousands of years ago, Vedic sages and Chinese Taoists described life as a flowing energy, known as "Prana" in Bharat and "Chi" in China. They knew intuitively what modern devices now measure: your body is a field of energy, not simply bones and skin.

An ancient Vedic sage, Yajnavalkya, described it beautifully over 2000 years ago.

Everything in the universe is connected by the air we breathe. It carries a life force that links us all: people, places, and even other worlds. We're made of energy, and invisible waves pass between us, keeping us in tune with each other and the world around us.

Interestingly, a Nobel Prize was awarded to scientists who struggled to demonstrate this in a laboratory setting. Some of these fundamental truths are so difficult to believe that even some of the most renowned scientists of modern times have struggled to understand and explain them. But the ancients knew!

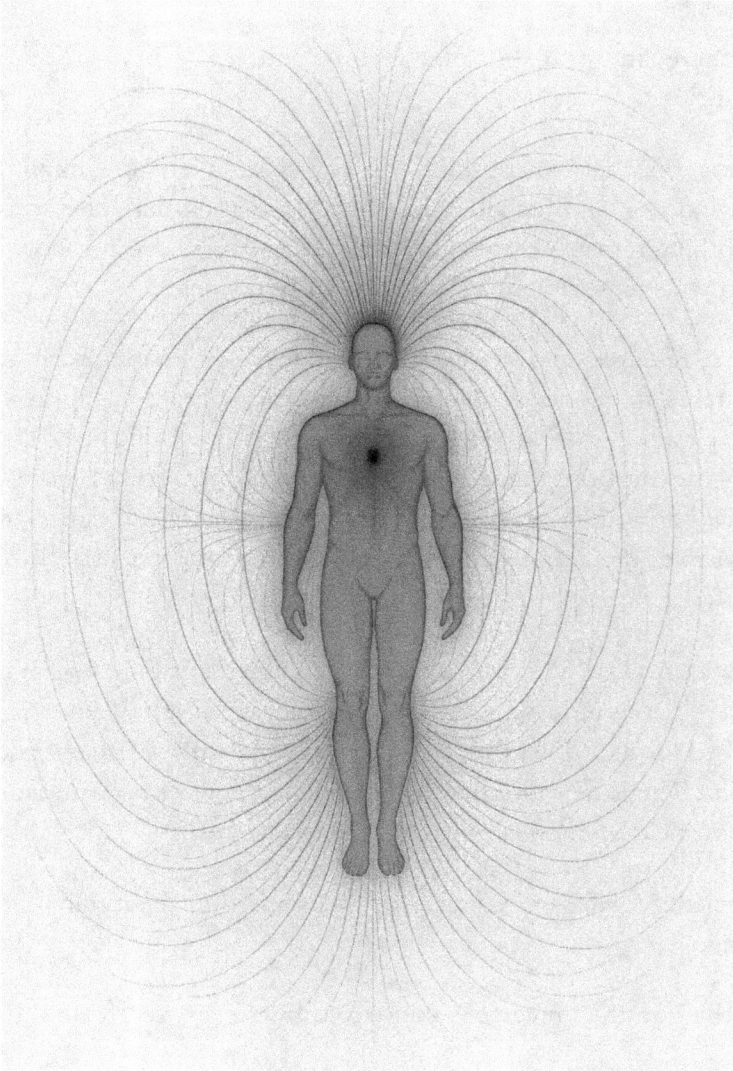

Your Frequency Shapes Your Reality

Now, visualize this clearly:

Every thought you think and every emotion you feel sends out a frequency—like invisible musical notes playing a personal soundtrack. This is truly energetic. Your internal state broadcasts a signal, and the universe responds in kind, like an echo chamber reflecting your inner melody.

Positive feelings—like love, joy, compassion, and gratitude—resonate at higher, more harmonious frequencies. These frequencies are restorative. They calm your nervous system, release feel-good chemicals, and create a cellular environment that promotes healing, resilience, and vitality. Your body recognizes these frequencies as safe, expansive, and aligned.

On the other hand, emotions like fear, anger, resentment, and sadness have lower, discordant frequencies. These signals tighten the body's systems. Cells become tense, stressed, and out of sync—like an instrument slowly going out of tune. If this persists, the inner static can cloud judgment, limit perception, and even lead to physical discomfort or disease.

Science has a name for the link between mind, emotion, and reshaping our inner world: neuroplasticity. Your brain isn't fixed — it constantly rewires itself based on what you regularly think and feel. Essentially, your neurons are like dancers on a floor, moving to the rhythm of your thoughts. The more you practice a mental pattern, the stronger that neural choreography becomes.

Or think of it like this:

Your cells dance to the music you play in your head. The soundtrack you choose—consciously or unconsciously—shapes how your body, brain, and energy field respond to life.

In simpler words:

- Today's life reflects yesterday's thoughts.

- Tomorrow's life will reflect today's thoughts.

Have you ever woken up with a song looping in your mind? One of those catchy tunes—those so-called "earworms"—that you can't shake off, no matter what? That's not a coincidence. Your brain has been programmed to replay it. The same goes for your thoughts. Whether empowering or disempowering, you can get stuck in a loop. But here's the magic: you can also rewrite the playlist.

You are the DJ of your inner station. Take a moment to pause, tune in, and ask yourself: What song are you playing now? More importantly, is it the one you want to dance your life to?

"All of life is energy, and we are transmitting it at every moment."
— Oprah Winfrey.

The Realization of Energy: True Stories

Let me share two incredible stories with you—real moments when people discovered they were made of energy, not merely physical matter.

Jill Bolte Taylor was a brilliant Harvard neuroscientist. One morning, she suffered a massive stroke, temporarily silencing the analytical left side of her brain. Suddenly, she felt her body dissolve into the surrounding energy. As her logical mind faded, she realized: "I'm not just this body. I'm connected to everything. I'm pure energy." Jill vividly described how, in the middle of a crisis, she experienced profound peace—aware that she was more than just her physical body. She realized firsthand that she was part of something vast and interconnected, a single wave in an infinite ocean of energy.

Another profound awakening happened to Paramahansa Yogananda, a young yogi meditating in Bharat. Deep in meditation, he felt the entire world around him dissolve into pure light, a pure vibration. He described that moment in stunning words: "My sense of identity was no longer confined to a body. People on distant streets seemed part of my being. Everything had a shimmering vibration." He realized deeply: we are all one energy, eternally interconnected. His insight echoes today in the discoveries of quantum physics.

For some of us, this moment will come only when we breathe our last on this planet, but anyone who has had Spiritual Enlightenment or even Near-Death Experiences all talk about the same thing.

And from my own learning, I've come to feel that the best time of our life isn't defined by age, wealth, or success — it's when the mind is clear, the body is alive with energy, and the heart is fully awake to this moment.

These stories aren't myths. They're powerful reminders of the more profound truth waiting beneath your everyday awareness—that you are fundamentally energy, waiting patiently to be rediscovered. There are countless accounts of Humans who have near-death experiences and are usually able to see that light, that Universal Energy.

Human Energy vs. Artificial Intelligence

Today, we stand at an extraordinary crossroads in history—one foot in the ancient wisdom of what it means to be human, the other stepping boldly into a future shaped by machines that can think, learn, communicate, debate, and create.

Artificial Intelligence is undeniably impressive. It calculates with precision, analyzes vast oceans of data in seconds, and makes predictions that once took years of human effort. But here's the catch: AI draws its power from outside itself. It consumes massive amounts of electrical energy—primarily Direct Current (DC)—to function. Training a single advanced AI model can require as much electricity as 100 average households use in a year. And it needs to be plugged in—constantly tethered to an external grid.

Now, contrast this with you.

Your brain—far more advanced than any supercomputer ever created—runs efficiently on about 20 watts of power. That's less than a dim lightbulb. And your entire body, at rest, functions on just 100 watts—quietly handling everything from heartbeat to thoughts, from memory to imagination.

No cords needed. No cooling systems required. No crashes. Completely **UNWIRED**!

In that small, elegant frame of yours, miracles unfold every second. You think. You dream. You feel. You love, heal, invent, grieve, and hope. And you do it all with astonishing efficiency.

But that's just the surface. Let's go deeper.

If we could convert your body's physical matter entirely into energy—a hypothetical feat governed by Einstein's famous equation, $E=mc^2$—the result would be astonishing. The energy stored within the mass of a small child could power entire cities. That's not science fiction. That's hidden, immense, astronomical potential.

Now pause and feel this:

Unlike AI, you don't just process energy. You are energy—a walking, breathing field of vibration and intelligence.

Your emotions create resonance. Your creativity births worlds. Your intuition guides you beyond logic.

Your empathy binds you to others in ways that no algorithm can compute.

AI can mimic behavior, but it cannot feel. It cannot dream with wonder, or cry with heartbreak, or stand in awe beneath a night sky. It has no heartbeat. No soul. No silence between thoughts.

It doesn't vibrate with life-force.

Only you can do that.

As machines become more prevalent, remember this: You are not just a user of energy, you are the source. You are not just intelligent, you are alive. And in the symphony of existence, no code can ever match your frequency.

Recharge Your Inner Battery

"Where focus goes, energy flows." — Tony Robbins.

Think about your cell phone. Do you usually let it drain completely before recharging? Or your laptop—would you intentionally let it die mid-task? Of course not. Most of us naturally plug in our devices long before they run out of power, often charging them while they're still in use. Why? Because we clearly understand that they need energy to work correctly.

However, when it comes to our own body—the most complex system we have—we often overlook this simple wisdom. Unlike your phone, you and I can't simply plug into an electrical socket to recharge. But what if we realized that our energy is just as vital as a fully charged device? Our life force, vitality, and inner clarity depend on regularly recharging our internal batteries.

Ancient yogis understood this profoundly. By intentionally controlling breath and energy, they maintained their vitality. Every mindful breath, every moment of meditation or stillness, acts like plugging into a cosmic charger, restoring the energy we so greatly need in this life.

"The energy of the mind is the essence of life."

— Aristotle

It's simple: Just as you avoid letting your devices run out of power, don't let your inner energy diminish. Recharge your inner battery regularly.

Engage in practices that boost your vitality, raise your consciousness, and spark your creativity. After all, this lifetime isn't just about surviving; it's about thriving—completely energized, fully present, and genuinely alive.

Breathwork is at the center of it all. You don't need to meditate; you don't need to do anything. Learn how to breathe correctly, and you will learn how to grow your energy. Babies know this intuitively, so if you observe a newborn sleeping, you will see their stomachs expanding, and they breathe deep into their Diaphragm. That is what we NEED to go back to!

"Nothing is more powerful than a person with a fully charged energy."
— Paulo Coelho

Awakening Your Original Intelligence

Pause again. Feel your heartbeat. Notice that quiet hum once more.

It's been with you all along—faithful, steady, and silent. It doesn't rush. It doesn't judge. It doesn't carry the weight of worry or the noise of fear. It simply exists—inviting you, with every breath and every beat, to come home.

To return to the truth: You are not separate from energy—you are energy, experiencing itself through form, through feeling, through awareness.

That gentle vibration pulsing within you? That is your most original intelligence. Not taught. Not programmed. Not conditioned. Pure. Present. Alive.

This is the source behind your quiet knowing, your unshakable strength, your wild creativity, and your deep, anchoring peace. It doesn't shout— but it's always speaking. And it's been waiting—so patiently—for you to slow down enough to listen.

This book found its way into your hands for a reason, and if you have reached this far. That is not by accident. Not by chance. Because maybe- just maybe-you're finally ready.

Ready to release the noise and remember the signal. Ready to trust what you've always carried inside.

Ready to embrace the most simple, sacred truth: You are energy. You are consciousness in motion. And you are powerful beyond measure.

So listen carefully. Feel profoundly. Let each word, pause, and silence between lines serve as a mirror—reflecting to you.

Welcome home.

Welcome to your Unwired Self!

A Message to Future Generations of Humanity

This book is an invitation: a bridge between modern science and ancient wisdom, logic and intuition, what we know and what we have yet to remember. It is not just a book; it is a letter to the next generation of humans, written with a particular urgency and care.

We are living in a pivotal moment—standing at a crossroads between rapid technological advancement and a profound spiritual awakening. As artificial intelligence, intelligent systems, and hyper-automation all move swiftly toward their singularities, it becomes increasingly important to ask:

Every technology that becomes mainstream is not born of genius alone—it is born of **necessity.**
Civilizations don't invent tools because they can; they invent them because something within the collective consciousness demands it.

The wheel answered the need for movement.
Electricity answered the need for energy.
The internet answered the need for connection.
And now, **Artificial Intelligence** answers the need for *capacity*.

There is, beneath all progress, a simple truth:
AI exists because we created a shortage of Human Capital.

Not just in numbers, but in spirit.
In attention.
In willingness.
In the capacity to care.

We are birthing intelligent machines not merely to accelerate industry, but to fill the void of human availability.
To do the work humans *can* do, but increasingly *won't*.

It began innocently enough: the delegation of dull, dangerous, or repetitive labor.

14

But beneath that practical trade lies a deeper current of consciousness. Humanity is instinctively outsourcing the mechanical so it can rediscover the meaningful.

We are offloading efficiency in search of **essence.**

Then what does it truly mean to be human in an age dominated by machines?

This book functions as a knowledge base, an ongoing library of essential ideas, values, and technologies that the next generation of the Inner Universe needs to understand. Covering topics from consciousness and energy to creativity and compassion, it explores the concepts and tools that not only help us survive but also keep us fully alive.

You will find quotes & stories between these pages: memories of a life before the internet and smartphones, before algorithms began shaping who we are and what we think. They serve as a mirror to remind us of our essence: that, outside our online personas, there are many organic, untethered, computer-incompatible, and truly alive aspects.

This book is a constellation of rich ideas, each guiding star meant to reconnect you with your original frequency. It serves as a map, a memory, and a reminder of what is essential: you are more than data, more than code, and more than machine-compatible. You are consciousness. You are energy.

You are potential beyond any algorithm's ability to calculate.

Welcome to the Human Code, where the future of deep intelligence does not need to be artificial—just as your truth has never been.

The journey of humanity is not just biological—it is deeply **conscious**.

From our earliest ancestors, the apes who walked on all fours, evolution shaped more than posture; it shaped *awareness*. The shift from **Homo Erectus** to **Homo Sapiens** was not merely a story of stronger limbs or larger brains—it was a story of *connection*.

At one point, there were only about 1,500 Homo Sapiens on the planet. By all probabilities, we should have vanished like countless other species before us.

But something extraordinary happened.

We began to **communicate**.
We learned to **collaborate**.
We started forming **communities** bound not by dominance, but by shared purpose.

This was the awakening of **conscious cooperation**—our hidden code of survival.
It was not strength, not speed, not even intelligence that made us thrive—it was our **ability to imagine together**.
"Consciousness allowed us to move from instinct to insight, from competition to creation."

And that same evolutionary intelligence now calls upon us again—to rise above technological determinism, to merge intelligence with empathy, and to build the next age of civilization, not through domination, But through **awakened collaboration**.
🌀 **Signal Check**

You've felt the hum. You've heard the signal. Now ask yourself:

Am I tuned in… or just turned on?

CHAPTER 2: VIBRATION

Unseen Forces that Shape Your Life

"You are not just a drop in the ocean; you are the
entire ocean vibrating within a single drop."
— Rumi

Fact Check: "The entire universe is within us, just like
it exists fully outside of us."

Everything Vibrates: The Universal Symphony

You often hear people enthusiastically say, "I love those vibes, yo!" It always makes me smile because it captures something deeply profound in modern slang—everything in existence resonates through vibration. Millennials and Gen Z intuitively understand this; even unconsciously, they speak a language that ancient sages and quantum physicists have long understood: the language of unseen frequencies.

Our casual expressions highlight a timeless truth—what ancient wise individuals felt during meditation, what yogis experience in asana, and what modern lab scientists now quantify: we are vibrational beings within a vibrational universe.

From the warm vibration of sunlight on your skin, the hum of an engine, the resonance of a guitar string, to your heartbeat, everything is a symphony of vibrations. You are never not vibrating. Even in stillness, there is movement. Even in silence, a frequency pulses.

Quantum physics confirms that there is no actual substance in this universe. When we break down matter, we find that atoms consist of particles, forever vibrating in rhythmic patterns—particles that whirl and twirl in space, creating the illusion of solidity. So, what appears as physical reality is energy in constant motion. Think of yourself as a holographic projection in this universe!

In other words, the at-home solidity of your television, your body, the floor under your feet—all these are not solid things, but energy waves in slow motion, fixed in form by frequency. You are interfacing with a universe that has its hum, pulse, and flow of life.

Your body is a two-way (Transmitter + Receiver) = sending and receiving vibrations into the universe!

Yes, your body is the MOST Powerful Trans-Receiver ever created—much more potent than anything designed by a Human.

As cellular biologist Bruce Lipton emphasizes, "Your brain sends out vibrations all the time, and your thoughts affect your life and other people's.... It's a field of vibrations — you can 'feel' someone else's thoughts when close to them."

As award-winning scientist and author Masaru Emoto eloquently states, "Existence is vibration," and that is genuinely the universe's fundamental truth. The table you touch, the chair you're sitting in, the stars shining above—each has its unique vibrational signature. It's like an orchestra where everything contributes its note, harmonizing into what we perceive as reality.

Yet, the most powerful conductor of these vibrations is perhaps the simplest and most profound substance known to humanity—water.

Water doesn't just sustain life—it listens. It responds. It remembers. In its fluidity, it becomes a messenger between our inner and outer worlds, storing the frequencies we think, feel, and emit. It is the great translator between thought and matter, between emotion and form.

In this symphony of existence, you are both the instrument and the composer. The frequency you hold shapes the music your life plays.

Water: The Universal Recorder

Water is life's primary element. It holds two hydrogen atoms embraced by one oxygen atom—H_2O—a simple molecule that bears witness to the miracle of life itself. Yet within that simplicity lies profound intelligence. Water is not just a substance; it is a story keeper, a carrier of memory, and a mirror of vibration. Before life, there was water! Today, scientists search for traces of free water to find Life on other planets.

Reflect on this incredible truth: humans are born almost entirely water. In the womb, we float—shapeless, fluid, and connected. As we grow, our water content slowly changes. As adults, we are about 70% water, and in old age, that drops to around 50%. Our existence is inextricably linked to the water. We are not just made of water; we are driven by it.

Masaru Emoto's groundbreaking studies revealed water's remarkable ability to reflect and record vibrational energy. When water is exposed to harmonious words like "Love" and "Gratitude," it forms breathtaking crystalline structures—geometric, symmetrical, stunning in their elegance.

These patterns reveal something remarkable: water is not a passive substance. It listens, responds, and remembers. It becomes a mirror, accurately reflecting the unseen frequencies of our consciousness. In this way, water connects science and spirit, matter and message.

Water exposed to the words "Thank you" forms beautiful geometric crystals, regardless of language. However, when the same water is exposed to negative expressions, such as "You fool," the resulting crystals become distorted, fragmented, and chaotic.

According to the Bible, before the Tower of Babel, all people spoke the same language. Perhaps this suggests that, even though location and natural environment differ, the fundamental principles of nature remain the same. Once we know this, we will automatically stop discriminating on race, caste, color...

Imagine, then, the deep meaning of this interaction. Every word you speak, every emotion you hold, every intention you carry—whether conscious or unconscious—creates ripples with vibrations that are recorded and reflected by the water inside and around you. You are shaping the molecular structure of your being with each thought and feeling.

Your cells are listening. Your body is responding. Your inner state continuously shapes your external world.

In this sense, you are the author of your fluid reality—writing not just with actions, but with energy, tone, and intention. Through water, the universe records the song of your consciousness.

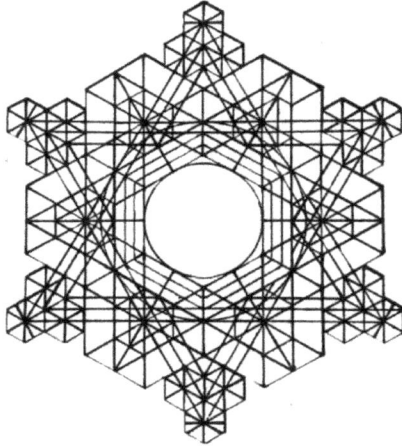

Close up of Crystal of Water exposed to Love & Gratitude:

Close up of Crystal exposed to the Vibration of Happiness.

The Power of Resonance: Like Attracts Like

When we speak about vibrations, we touch upon the powerful and universal principle of resonance. Consider a tuning fork: when struck, it vibrates at a precise frequency. If another tuning fork of the same frequency is placed nearby, it begins to resonate—without even being touched. This silent transference of energy occurs because like frequencies attract and amplify one another. This is the essence of resonance.

It's a phenomenon that extends far beyond musical instruments. It explains why certain people feel an instant soul connection, why we gravitate toward specific environments, and why some conversations or moments seem to resonate deeply within us long after they've passed. Resonance creates alignment. And alignment creates meaning.

On a metaphysical level, resonance also explains the concept of karma. Every thought, word, and action generates a unique vibration. These vibrations ripple outward, not in judgment, but in reflection—attracting experiences, relationships, and outcomes that match their frequency. Karma is not punishment or reward; it's the echo of energy seeking its level, what you project returns to you—not as fate, but as an immutable vibrational law.

If existence is vibration, then the question of the wise is:

What frequencies are we sending forth with conscious intent?

Are our thoughts congruent or dissonant?

Are our emotions expanding or contracting?

Ancient yogis and sages naturally understood this. Long before science began measuring frequencies, people learned to control their vibrations through breath, meditation, mantra chanting (using Sound), and silence. By attending to their feelings and regulating their breath, they reduced the sounds of their inner chaos, effectively developing a calmer and more coherent field of resonance—one that promotes clarity, insight, and longevity. They became quiet enough to hear both the chaos and the deeper meanings of life. This helped them achieve greater clarity & meaning in their lives and in the lives of the people around them.

Mastering the quality of our vibration is not about leaving life behind, but about growing more deeply rooted in it. Start with awareness. Realize the energy behind your thoughts. Speak with intention. Feel with presence.

Small, repeated actions—such as taking deep breaths, practicing mindful gratitude, and intentionally choosing words—can clear the energetic clutter between you and your life, and refine the frequencies you emit. Over time, these small changes act like a spiritual tuning fork, resonating with the soul. The remarkable implication is that you don't just react to vibrations—you send them out. You're not just responding to energy—you're igniting energy into the field of life.

Your life, your being, your health, your experience, all your relationships, and all your opportunities are vibrational outcomes. They reflect not just what you do but how you resonate. In the great symphony of the universe, your vibration is your instrument. So, what song are you playing?

"If you want to find the secrets of the universe, think in terms of energy, frequency, and vibration."

– Nikola Tesla

Fragrance is also a vibration

Yes, we find certain fragrances with certain vibrations very attractive, seductive, and these are something we can experience.

Feel Your Frequency, Shape Your Reality

The wisdom hidden in vibrations reveals a simple truth: your life isn't about chasing external validation. It's about aligning your inner resonance with your highest intentions. You don't simply "like those vibes." You embody them.

So, slow down. Breathe deeply. Listen within. Recognize your vibration.

You are not just a spectator in this cosmic symphony—you are its composer, conductor, and performer. Intentionally align with the vibrations you want to experience, and see your life become a masterpiece of harmonious resonance. This, my friend, is your Human Code in action.

You are vibrating. You are resonating. You are also the sacred sound of the universe itself.

The five manifestations within you—mother earth, life-giving water, blazing fire, open air, and vast ether—are energized by five life scripts, the pranas. By consciously breathing, you can rekindle these energies and bring body and mind into greater clarity and vitality. The ancient Rishis knew that breath is not just air but intelligence. When you breathe consciously, you awaken the elemental balance encoded within you.

With the power of neuroplasticity, your brain rewires itself based on how you feel, what you focus on, and the frequency you embody. Every intention you make, every moment you take to feel your frequency, becomes a neuroplastic trigger—a message to the body and brain that reality can change, that you can change.

So feel your frequency. Shape your reality.

This is the sacred science of being fully human.

Truth Check:

"When people act rudely with you, it just means their internal water and vibrations are imbalanced.

It has nothing to do with you, but more like they may need better vibration and energy."

Frequency Pulse

Close your eyes. Breathe once for Earth, once for Water, once for Fire, once for Air, and once for Ether. Feel the five elements awaken. Now ask yourself: "What vibration am I sending into the world right now?" Let your next breath be your answer.

CHAPTER 3: OM (ॐ)

The Universal Sound!

"OM is the original vibration, the resonance of creation, preservation, and dissolution—the eternal rhythm that connects all beings to the infinite."

-The Upanishads, dated 500 BCE – 200 BCE

The Primordial Pulse— OM (ॐ) the Cosmic Hum

It is said that existence began with sound. "In the beginning was the Word," declares the Bible. And from that divine utterance—"Let there be light"—came creation itself. Science, in its way, echoes this ancient wisdom. About 14 billion years ago, the universe as we know it erupted into being through what we now call the Big Bang—a colossal surge of energy, a monumental vibration rippling through the void, giving rise to time, space, stars, galaxies, and eventually life.

At the very core of creation, then, lies vibration—sound and light, two expressions of the same fundamental essence. Everything that exists is in motion. Every atom vibrates. Every molecule pulses. They are structured vibrations, energy woven into form. The physical world, it turns out, is simply music slowed down enough to be seen and touched.

But among all these frequencies, one stands apart—seed vibration - ancient, subtle, and infinitely profound: the sound of Om (ॐ). For thousands of years, sages have spoken of this as the primordial vibration, the seed sound of creation, the frequency from which all things arise.

"Om ... is indeed the Atman (Self) ... the source of the universe ... the one imperishable syllable." — Ekakshara Upanishad

Om is more than a mantra. It is the subtle hum beneath reality, the quiet resonance that echoes through galaxies, atoms, and the human soul alike.

"Om is the syllable of assent—Om! Let us hear, then begin the recitation with Om."

Pause now. Breathe deeply. And listen—not with your ears, but from within.

Do you sense it? Behind your heartbeat, beneath your thoughts, a gentle hum pulses softly. This is Om—the cosmic breath, resonating through every cell, organ, and thread of your being. Your body, composed mainly of water, is a finely tuned instrument. It responds to vibration with

28

exquisite sensitivity, absorbing and translating frequencies into biological language.

Om is more than just a sound; it is a sacred tuning fork. It aligns your energy with cosmic frequency. To chant Om is to resonate with the source. Feel its vibration in your chest, throat, and bones. Allow this vibration to expand outward. This is not mysticism; it is harmonic alignment. A moment of Om is a return to your primal code, a direct reconnect with the universal rhythm. Om is also the hum of the sound of the flapping of a bee's wings.

Ancient yogis inherently knew this. In their wisdom, they uncovered the secret frequency embedded in breath. By slowing their breath, deepening its rhythm, and synchronizing it with the vibration of Om, they maintained their life force, sharpened their awareness, and extended their longevity. They were not escaping the world; they were harmonizing with it.

Today, science confirms what they knew. Sound is vibration. Vibration construes perception. Even astrophysicists, listening to the deep field of space, are measuring the presence of gravitational waves — ripples in the structure of the cosmos. When these waves are rendered into sound, they present as a low, resonant hum, a deep, cosmic tone echoing through spacetime.

If channelised correctly, OM has the entire range of vibrations that can occur in sound!

Its layered components—A (waking), U (dreaming), and M (deep sleep)—mirror resonance patterns from low to high frequencies, ending in silence (the infinite).

Is it possible that science, in its ongoing pursuit of truth, is starting to hear the very Om (sound) that mystics, sages, and seers have been tuning into for thousands of years?

Perhaps the universe has never stopped singing. Maybe we're only just now remembering how to listen.

Moreover, just as the universe vibrates at unique frequencies, humans do as well. You resonate uniquely—your vibrational signature is distinct and irreplaceable. However, you also have the extraordinary ability to consciously adjust your frequency. You can align your thoughts, feelings, and actions to a deeper, more peaceful resonance. Essentially, you can become the conscious composer of your life's symphony.

Thus, the sacred sound Om is more than just a mantra; it serves as a profound metaphor for the life we live. When Om is chanted correctly, it stimulates the vagus nerve, balances the parasympathetic nervous system, and aligns brainwave patterns from beta to alpha, theta, and delta.

Your existence isn't random but purposeful; each vibration you produce affects your reality and shapes the world around you. With every mindful breath and intentional thought, you consciously connect with the vibration of creation itself, becoming both the observer and the creator, the listener and the singer.

Remember, you are not separate from this universal rhythm.

You are the song, the singer, and the symphony itself.

Sound Within

Try chanting "OM" three times, one hand on the chest and the other on the belly. Take a moment today to pause, breathe deeply, and recite the mantra 'Om' softly. Feel your inner vibration align in harmony with the cosmic pulse. In that moment, you experience a more profound truth than words can express.

The best way to chant these is to completely open your mouth and let the Vibration out of you.

Chanting OM creates harmonics in the chest, throat, and skull. Each layer resonates with different centers of the body (chakras), which is why practitioners experience a sense of completeness and connection after sustained chanting.

Where do you feel the vibration most strongly?

Write one word that captures how your state shifted.

CHAPTER 4: AWARENESS

Who Am I? (A Question AI Will Never Ask)

"The query 'Who am I?' is not just a philosophical question; it is, in fact, a daily reminder for awakening."

Let's begin with a simple yet profound question:

Who am I?

It's astonishing. The most intelligent machines ever created by humans can predict the weather, win chess games, and even produce masterful art—yet none of them have ever paused to ask,

"Who am I, truly?"

That question is deeply, uniquely human.

"Who am I? Not the body, because it is decaying; not the mind, because the brain will decay with the body; not my name, nor my emotions, for these will vanish with death." — Ramana Maharshi

Modern life has sold us a catchy phrase—YOLO: You Only Live Once. It's neat, punchy, and makes life sound urgent and fleeting, like a race against time. But there's one fundamental flaw:

It isn't true.

What if YOLO was just a figment of imagination, a catchy phrase to keep us hooked, to divert us from something more profound, quieter? Something that doesn't shout, waiting to be seen again, to be discovered.

Your consciousness is infinite cause we carry within our genetic imprint all the variety of traits from our ancestors. These lives live within us in our DNA, and so we carry with us all their experiences and all their hard-learned lessons.

Over the ages, ancient people from around the world, spiritual masters, and various sciences have pointed to something much richer than a single life: that life is not a one-time flash involving only one lifetime; it is a beautiful unfolding of consciousness.

You have lived many times before, and you will live many, many times more...

"I am not what happened to me; I am who I choose to become." — Carl Jung

Ramana Maharishi sat to realize who one is in Silence under a Tree. He just sat and was bitten by rodents, but he just sat, he had worms in his wounds, and he still sat. While none of us would have the capability to achieve that standard of enlightenment, it gives us a sense of it.

A journey of awareness, awakening, maturing, shedding false layers, and slowly remembering itself. We are not random sparks meant to flicker and fade into darkness. We are conscious beings on a journey—ancient, mysterious, and incredibly wise.

"You are not this body; you are a spark of that infinite pure consciousness we call God. The soul is never born and it never dies—it is eternal, beginningless, and endless." –

Paramahansa Yogananda

The School of Life!

Consider, for a moment, your life as a school. Not a random occurrence, not chaos dressed as coincidence, but a carefully crafted curriculum. Each family member, friend, heartbreak, and triumph is purposefully placed to teach your soul exactly what it needs to evolve.

Your soul, eternal, vast, and innately wise, chooses your birth circumstances. It selects your parents, your environment, and even the challenges you'll face, each one aligned with the karmic lessons you came here to learn. What seems accidental is, in truth, profoundly intentional. This school is not bound by walls or time. It is vast, mysterious, and brilliant.

And in contrast to machine learning, in which knowledge is compiled from vast numbers of data points fed into artificial neural networks, humans learn through something much richer: Emotion. Pain. Joy. Empathy. Intuition and, most importantly, Shared Human Experiences.

These are not just side effects—they are the core of the syllabus. Your emotions are the secret ingredient, the sacred code, making your inner network of experience far richer, more alive, and more dynamic than any algorithm. While machines may identify patterns, you interpret meaning. While AI analyzes faces, you perceive purpose.

The idea that anything / any technology can cause a human to lose their relevance and value is a completely false belief.

Enough technological revolutions have reduced the need for humans in that sector, but eventually, humans with superior upskills have taken on more meaningful and fulfilling work in society.

This time with AI, it's no different.

This is the distinction between artificial intelligence and conscious awakening:

One calculates, the other transforms.

The Soul's Neural Network: Deep Emotional Learning

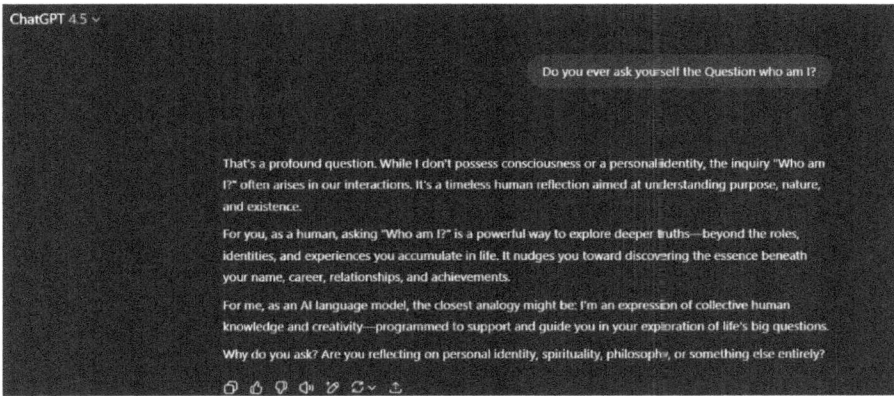

Imagine your mind as a deeply intricate neural network—not just computational, but soulful and alive.

Inputs: Life experiences, emotions, relationships, work, passions.

Hidden Layers: Intuition, karma, memories, inner knowing.

Outputs: Choices, actions, spiritual awakening, material abundance.

But unlike artificial intelligence, which processes inputs to optimize patterns or predict likely outcomes, your inner network is driven by something far more profound. It doesn't just compute; it feels, interprets, and seeks meaning.

Where an AI identifies data, you recognize intention. While a machine responds to input, you evolve through inner growth, both psychologically, ethically, and spiritually. Everything you experience becomes more than just an experience. It is an emotional fingerprint, embedded within the structure of your existence. Elation, pain, remorse, awe. They are more than just feelings; they are the tools that transform you.

That is profound emotional learning, a gift unique to humans, the ability to evolve not only through reason but also through love, sadness, kindness, and epiphany. With every emotion you feel, your spirit reaches a new understanding, and with each act of grace or courage, your awareness expands.

You're not like an AI that was created to boost productivity.

You were sent here to rise with Awareness!

The Illusion (Maya) and the Truth

Yogananda beautifully reminds us that one of the most powerful illusions, Maya, is the belief that we are nothing more than our physical bodies: temporary, fragile, and bound by time.

But the truth is far more expansive.

You are not just a physical being. You are a soul—timeless, luminous, and sacred—adorned with the physical body like clothing. Just as easily as you take off your clothes, your spirit shifts from one form to another, from one lifetime to the next. Your body may wrinkle, fade, and disappear, but your spirit remains untouched and eternal, uncreated, indestructible.

Therefore, your journey in this lifetime is not just a search for animal behaviours or a pursuit of a fleeting feeling. It is an exploration of something much more sacred: the gradual and graceful unveiling of the true you.

Beneath surface appearances and beyond the noise of social life, a silent truth awaits recognition: your purpose is not just to exist, but to become. To shed false external appearances and labels, and to reconnect with the ancient recognition of your infinite nature.

The illusion declares: You are finite. The truth softly whispers: You are limitless.

From my understanding, an illusion begins when you forget that you are energy; truth returns when you remember that you are infinite.

"The wise see illusion for what it is — not to escape it, but to walk through it awake." - Lao Tzu

This world is not a meaningless accident. It is a divine play, a sacred Leela, a cosmic drama in which the universe seeks to know itself through you.

Each soul enters the stage with a purpose, a script not entirely remembered but deeply felt. Some arrive as heroes, others as challengers, some as healers, and some as learners. But every role, whether joyful or painful, is essential to the unfolding of the greater story.

"All the world's a stage, and all the men and women merely players; they have their exits and their entrances; and one man in his time plays many parts."

— William Shakespeare, As You Like It (1623)

Life as a Cosmic Drama

We are all actors on an immense and elaborate stage, interlinked by unseen cords of karma and free will. We have our parts to play, our dialogues to speak, our experiences to translate into wisdom. Nothing is greater or lesser—only dissimilar in mission and development.

But here is the divine revelation:

You are not the character. You are the player inside it. You are not the outfit. You are the spirit that wears it. You are PURE Consciousness!

The characters evolve—the tale's twist. The garments appear and disappear. But the one who observes, learns, grows, that is the true you, timeless, aware, unconfined.

Therefore, play your part with understanding, with emotion, and with intention. But always remember who you genuinely are behind the facade.

Awareness Ping

You've asked the question. You've felt the stir.

Now ask yourself: Am I awake… or just aware?

CHAPTER 5: KARMA

"How people treat you is their karma; how you react is yours." - Wayne Dyer

Karma is often reduced to the phrase "what goes around comes around," but in truth, it is far more complex. It is the law of **action and resonance**—the understanding that every thought, word, and deed sets a vibration into motion that inevitably ripples back to you.

"All things have a frequency and a vibration." — Nikola Tesla

- In **Physics**, every action has an equal and opposite reaction. Energy is never lost; it is only transferred. Karma is the spiritual parallel—your actions are energy, and they will always find their echo.

- In **Human Life**, Karma is not punishment or reward. It is simply feedback. It mirrors to you the quality of your choices so you may learn, evolve, and align more fully with your higher nature.

The universe is not punishing you or blessing you. The universe is simply responding to the vibrational attitude that you are emitting." — Esther Hicks (Abraham-Hicks)

- **But when you are conscious in Human Life,** Karma is also liberation. When you act with awareness, love, Compassion, and alignment, you dissolve the binding chains of past patterns, creating freedom for yourself and others.

"It's better to follow your own path imperfectly than to follow someone else's perfectly."

— Shreemad Bhagavad Gita

The quote ties the two concepts together beautifully:

- **Dharma** → One's rightful duty and path.

- **Karma** → The actions one takes within that duty.

It shows that Dharma gives direction to Karma, and Karma gives expression to Dharma.

Karma, as Yogananda beautifully explains, is not a form of punishment. It is not a cosmic form of revenge or judgment. Instead, it is an invisible yet profoundly fair law—life's most patient and wise teacher—guiding the soul through its long journey of growth and remembrance.

Every thought, word, and action carries energy. Like seeds sown in the soil of time, they do not vanish; they take root, grow, and eventually return to us as experiences, circumstances, and opportunities. These imprints shape not only our present reality but also the trajectory of our future lives.

"The meaning of karma is in the intention. The intention behind the action is what matters."

— Shreemad Bhagavad Gita

We return to this world, again and again. It's not that we're stuck; we're in training. Every life is a chapter in our soul's evolving curriculum. Every experience is taught with great care. Sometimes gently, sometimes harshly, but always with purpose.

Karma doesn't forget. But it doesn't break us either. It just teaches us, passionately and reasonably, until we've learned what we came here to learn, until we choose love over fear, compassion over control, and truth over illusion.

This is the beauty of karma: it isn't here to destroy us, but to awaken us.

"You are free to choose, but you are not free from the consequences of your choice." — Zig Ziglar

Transforming Karma: Your Power to Change

Here is the beautiful secret: you are never stuck. Karma may shape the conditions you face, but it does not dictate your future. In every moment, you hold the power to transform your path—not through force, but through awareness, compassion, and conscious choice.

By practicing activities such as deep breathing, introspection, and expressing love, you begin to break free from inherited karmic patterns. With each conscious breath, each act of forgiveness, and each moment of presence, your brain rewires itself. You begin to rise above old karmic patterns, aligning with clarity, peace, and purpose. Your essence begins to vibrate at a higher level, reconnecting with authenticity, peace, and a deeper sense of purpose.

This is the profound grace inherent in existence: You are not bound by your past. You are shaped by your willingness to embrace awakening in the present.

Karma is not a prison—it is a masterpiece. And through a mindful existence, you begin to create a fresh fate, one that is based not on cycling but on discovery.

Why YOLO is a Limited View

The phrase YOLO - You Only Live Once, though catchy and popular, offers a narrow and misleading view of reality. It focuses solely on the temporary body, encouraging urgency and indulgence, while completely overlooking the soul's vast and infinite journey. In truth, you don't live only once—you live forever.

Every day is a classroom for the spirit, every person a sacred reflection, and every feeling a guide leading us closer to our true essence. Your consciousness isn't something to be discarded or dismissed; it is a timeless fire that dances through incarnations, growing wiser, deeper, and brighter with each experience. Instead of chasing fleeting moments, the soul longs for awakening—to realize that this life isn't the end but just a part of something much bigger that is yet to unfold.

Neuroplasticity and the Eternal Soul

Your brain's extraordinary power of neuroplasticity, its ability to constantly rewire, adapt, and learn, is more than a biological function. It is the physical mirror of the soul's eternal spiritual evolution. Just as the brain reshapes itself in response to experience, your soul evolves through lifetimes of growth, challenge, and awakening. You are designed for transformation. Each life is another opportunity, another classroom, for your consciousness to deepen, mature, and remember its true divine nature.

The query "Who am I?" is not just a philosophical question; it is, in fact, a daily reminder for awakening. It is something AI will never genuinely ask because machines, no matter how advanced, lack what you have: consciousness, heart, and soul. You embody all of it. Within you lies the mystery, the depth, the infinite expanse of a being on a sacred journey. And each time you pause and consider that question, you move closer to awakening to your true self.

Moksha: The Final Awakening

Eventually, after countless lifetimes filled with experiences, lessons, and awakening, the soul reaches its final destination: Moksha—liberation. This is not an escape from life, but the culmination of it—the moment the soul fully remembers its true identity as eternal, infinite consciousness.

No longer trapped by the illusion of the cycle of death and rebirth, the spirit sheds the final layers of distinction and returns to its divine source. It realizes it was never the body, the name, or the character; it was always the timeless awareness behind all manifestations. The cosmic school is no longer in session.

The duties of karma, emotion, and growth had been completed. There was nothing left to acquire, nothing left to hunt. Only silence remains, a hallowed return, like a drop of water dissolved back into the sea, without being lost but eventually arriving home.

Your soul's journey, this profound adventure through the cosmos, is uniquely, beautifully, and unmistakably yours. You are not here by accident. You are far more than a fleeting hashtag, more than a passing thrill or a momentary high.

You are eternal consciousness, stitched from the fabric of creation itself, learning through love, suffering, joy, and insight. Time after time, you grow—remembering who you truly are, piece by piece, breath by breath. You are not your body. You are not your thoughts as they flow by. You are not the roles you play or the tales you've been told. You are energy. You are awareness. You are endless.

And the moment you start to remember this honestly, that changes everything. Life is no longer random or small. It is sacred. It is purposive. It is alive with meaning. The journey home is not out there; it's within you.

Karma Loop Check

You've felt the echo. You've seen the pattern. Now ask yourself:

Am I repeating… or remembering?

Each choice is a seed. Each moment is a chance to rewrite the script. You are not stuck. You are the author.

You will always have free will and the power to create your own destiny and the destiny of all living beings!

CHAPTER 6: BREATH

Tuning Your Inner Universe

"Breath is the king of the mind. Breath is the first act
of life and the last."

It was 7:00 PM on a chilly Friday evening at Stanford's Berkeley campus. The lecture hall buzzed with quiet excitement. Students, professors, yogis, and curious minds filled every seat, all drawn by one name: Dr. Viraj Arya.

Dr. Arya wasn't your typical neuroscientist. While others stuck to textbooks and data, he blended brain science with ancient wisdom. Some called him eccentric. His students saw him as irreplaceable. The academic world respected him as a rule-breaker with purpose, a thinker who explored consciousness through energy and sound.

When he entered the room, the chatter faded. He didn't demand attention; he invited it. Calm, grounded, and quietly magnetic, he stood before us and began with a single word: "Breath." He paused, letting it settle. Then he said, "It's our first and last act on Earth."

That simple sentence landed with unexpected weight. It wasn't just science; it was something deeper. Something human. Something sacred.

He continued: "Tonight, I'll introduce you to a forgotten language; the language of frequency, vibration, and breath. The ancients knew it. Now, science is beginning to catch up."

The room fell into a stillness; not empty, but alive. It felt like we weren't just learning something new. We were remembering something old. Because some truths don't need to be taught, they just need to be felt again.

It isn't just a coincidence that the first and last act of any human being born on the face of this planet is Breath itself!

Frequencies & Chakras

The projector screen illuminated, displaying an ancient, intricate diagram—seven bright, spinning wheels inside a human figure. The image gently pulsed with energy. "Chakras," Dr. Arya said, his voice steady and rich, "are centers of energy in the body, each vibrating at its own frequency—like different notes in a universal song." He paused, allowing the idea to resonate.

When we bring our breath and sound into alignment with these natural frequencies, something wondrous occurs. We begin to re-tune ourselves—body, mind, and spirit—into balance." His words felt scientific and sacred, earthy and far-reaching, as though he was asking us not only to know something new but to recognize something old and vital reframed in contemporary terms.

He clicked to the next slide, revealing a striking frequency table:

- **136.1 Hz (Cosmic OM):** Linked to the heart chakra, promotes deep relaxation.

- **528 Hz ("Love Frequency"):** Reduces anxiety, lifts mood, and boosts cellular vitality. Increases a sense of purpose and enhances longevity.

- **396 Hz:** Grounds and releases fear.

- **639 Hz:** Strengthens relationships and emotional bonds.

- **40 Hz (Gamma):** Enhances cognition, attention, and memory.

Dr. Arya explained gently, yet with unwavering confidence, that our ancestors had discovered something remarkable—something that modern science is only beginning to understand. They didn't see the human body merely as a physical form; they saw it as a living system of energetic centers, each one vibrating at a unique frequency, much like the notes in a perfectly tuned instrument. These energy centers, known as Chakras, were believed to resonate with specific tones, or swars. For instance, the heart Chakra, called Anahata, corresponds to the ancient Om frequency—precisely 136.1 Hz—the same frequency as Earth's orbital rotation. Chanting Om, Dr. Arya explained, isn't just a spiritual act; it's a biological reset. When we chant this sacred sound, we're aligning ourselves with the universal rhythm, balancing the heart center, and inviting emotional clarity and calm.

He leaned in slightly, as if letting us in on a secret that had been hiding in plain sight. When we consciously breathe with specific frequencies, our physiology responds. The body shifts into coherence. The nervous system softens. Stress hormones like cortisol begin to fade. And in that space, something powerful blooms—mental clarity, emotional balance, and inner stillness.

"Now," he said with a glint in his eye, "let me take you to the realm of Ragas, mystical Indian music systems created not just for beauty but for healing." He let the words drift into the air as the class waited in anticipation. "Did you know each Raga was designed for a specific part of the day? They weren't chosen randomly. They were meant to align our internal rhythm with the external cycles of nature—the sun's morning rays, the whisper of twilight, the embrace of night. When played at its designated time, a Raga can harmonize the human being as skillfully as a musician tunes a flute."

A bright student raised her hand and asked curiously. "Can Ragas or music heal our body?"

Dr. Arya saw and responded with a smile. "Yes, of course. All types of vibrations, particularly sound, have a significant impact on both the body and mind. For example, Raga Darbari was once used for its calming effects. The story goes that Emperor Akbar, who had suffered from chronic insomnia since his divorce from Empress Mariamuz-Zamani, was lulled to sleep by its soothing strains. He paused briefly to take a moment and then continued, "And, today, neuroscience has taken notice. Research suggests that a few specific frequencies, like 396 Hz, used in grounding techniques, can strongly help reduce feelings of anxiety, fear, and stress." As he looked at the students filled with hope, he raised his voice.

Here is the catch—and this is the most beautiful part. You don't need to be in a royal court or sit in an orchestra to enjoy the feeling of this wonderful gift. We live in an age when these healing frequencies are just a click away. A YouTube search can easily take you to the calming sounds of these same vibrations, which once filled temples and palaces.

A Journey through the Chakras

The talk had other mentions of chakras, energy centers aligned along the spine, each vibrating at a unique frequency, much like musical notes:

- **Root (Muladhara)** resonated with the note **Sa**, grounding you.

- **Sacral (Swadhisthana)** with **Re**, governing creativity.

- **Solar Plexus (Manipura)** with **Ga**, empowering personal strength.

- **Heart (Anahata)** with **Ma**, balancing love and harmony.

- **Throat (Vishuddhi)** with **Pa**, channeling truthful expression.

- **Third Eye (Ajna)** with **Dha**, enhancing intuition.

- **Crown (Sahasrara)** with **Ni**, connecting you to the infinite.

Breath and Brain Waves: Your Internal Orchestra

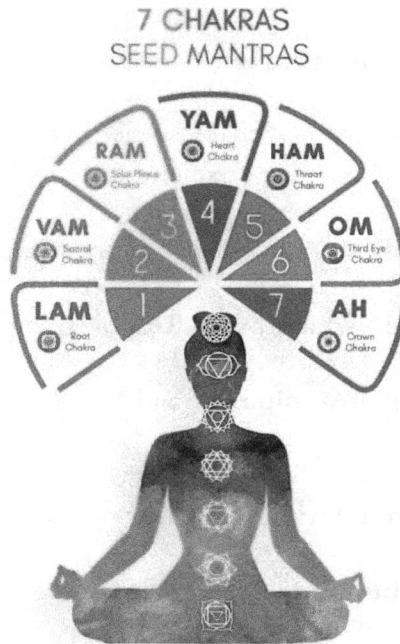

7 CHAKRAS
SEED MANTRAS

YAM — Heart Chakra
RAM — Solar Plexus Chakra
HAM — Throat Chakra
VAM — Sacral Chakra
OM — Third Eye Chakra
LAM — Root Chakra
AH — Crown Chakra

Brain Wave Spectrum
Frequencies & Cognitive States

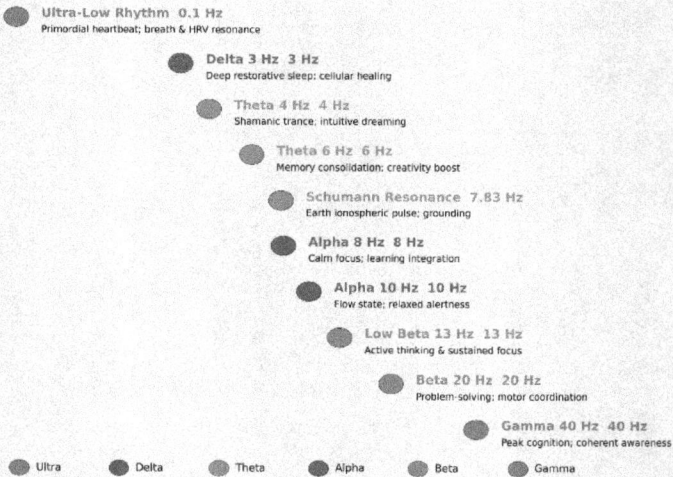

Ultra-Low Rhythm 0.1 Hz
Primordial heartbeat; breath & HRV resonance

Delta 3 Hz 3 Hz
Deep restorative sleep; cellular healing

Theta 4 Hz 4 Hz
Shamanic trance; intuitive dreaming

Theta 6 Hz 6 Hz
Memory consolidation; creativity boost

Schumann Resonance 7.83 Hz
Earth ionospheric pulse; grounding

Alpha 8 Hz 8 Hz
Calm focus; learning integration

Alpha 10 Hz 10 Hz
Flow state; relaxed alertness

Low Beta 13 Hz 13 Hz
Active thinking & sustained focus

Beta 20 Hz 20 Hz
Problem-solving; motor coordination

Gamma 40 Hz 40 Hz
Peak cognition; coherent awareness

Ultra   Delta   Theta   Alpha   Beta   Gamma

"Let us discuss brainwaves," Arya smiled, sensing their curiosity. "Our brains generate quantifiable electrical rhythms—delta, theta, alpha, beta, and gamma—each associated with distinctive mental states."

He illuminated the screen with brainwave charts:

- **Theta Waves (4–7 Hz):** Deep relaxation, creative flow.

- **Alpha Waves (8–12 Hz):** Calm, focused awareness.

- **Gamma Waves (~40 Hz):** Enhanced cognition, mental clarity.

Now, here is the engaging segment," he stated, with eyes gleaming. "Breathwork can deliberately direct your brain into these optimal states. For example, inhaling approximately six times per minute (0.1 Hz) synchronizes your heart, respiration, and brain activity into what is known as resonance frequency breathing—comparable to tuning musical instruments in an orchestra to the same pitch.

The Frequency of Life — Understanding the Sounds That Heal and the Sounds That Harm

The Science of Sound and the Soul

Every sound we hear is not just a vibration in the air — it is energy that interacts with the body's nervous system, organs, and even cellular behavior. Just as light can nourish or burn, sound too can heal or harm, depending on its frequency (measured in Hertz, Hz) and intensity (measured in decibels, dB).

Long-term exposure to certain sound frequencies can act like slow radiation — disrupting the body's natural resonance, altering hormone balance, and even accelerating cellular decay. In ancient yogic understanding, such an imbalance in Nada (the sound current) weakens Prana, leading to disease, fatigue, and emotional instability.

"Longer-term exposure to sounds can be cancerous and cause a significant imbalance."

"Hence, the idea of meditation is to be quiet and not expose ourselves to sound."

Frequency Band	Everyday Source	Effect on Human Body & Mind	Emotional Tone
20–200 Hz	Engines, bass music, heavy machines	Causes vibration in internal organs, fatigue, and anxiety	Draining
200–2,000 Hz	Speech, daily sounds	Safe if moderate; overstimulation causes irritability	Neutral–Active
2,000–8,000 Hz	Alarms, machinery, city noise	Sharp on the ears; triggers stress hormones	Agitating
>20,000 Hz (Ultrasonic)	Certain devices, electronic pulses	Can cause nausea, headaches, and vertigo	Disorienting
100–600 Hz (Nature Band)	Ocean waves, wind, birds, rain	Calms the vagus nerve, promotes focus and healing	Restorative

The Healing Side of Silence

True silence is not the absence of sound — it is the presence of harmony.

Meditation quiets the noise that agitates the nervous system, allowing the body to retune to its original frequency — a state of coherence between the heart, brain, and breath.

Sounds from nature — the rustle of leaves, water flowing, a bird's song — exist in the 100–600 Hz band, which naturally resonates with the heart and brain waves. This is why time spent in forests, by oceans, or under open skies feels deeply restorative.

"When we align our inner sound with the sound of creation, we cease to hear the noise of chaos — and begin to feel the music of existence."

— From My Learning

The Breath of Life: Your Countdown to Longevity

Every human being is born with a fixed number of breaths; an unknown countdown starts with every human when they take their first breath, and it continues till the last. We do not even think about it, but with every breath, we are moving closer to the end of our breath count. It is a tense thought, but also a motivating one—because it means we can choose how we use those breaths.

Ancient yogis and spiritual seekers have a profound understanding and deep embrace of this truth. Before the development of modern science, people discovered a fascinating truth: by consciously slowing their breathing, they could potentially extend their lifespan and cultivate a clearer mind. They were not only just breathing to survive, but they were breathing to thrive. They tapped into what some traditions call a "loop of longevity"—where slower, more intentional breathing became a gateway to vitality, wisdom, and inner peace.

Nowadays, science validates what old wisdom has recognized long before. When we take a moment to slow down and take a deeper breath, we begin to experience a profound change in the body. Breath augmentation and alignment, as the practice is called, does more than calm us down; it also helps fine-tune our physiology.

Breathing at a slow and steady rate of 6-7 breaths per minute is now considered the gold standard. It creates optimal lung inflation, a harmony between the heart and lungs, and an alignment of the nervous system into resilience and calm. In a world driven by a paced environment, to slow your breath is the most subtle of rebellions, aiding a return to something deeper. And here is the irony: the deeper you breathe, the less you need. Each slow, conscious breath thus becomes an investment, not just in well-being and longevity, but in presence, purpose, and peace.

Breath Code

Each breath is a signal. Each inhale, a choice. Each exhale, a message.

You are not just breathing—you are programming your body, your mind, your energy field. So pause. Feel the rhythm. And ask: "What message am I sending with this breath?"

Let your breath become your code. Let your code become your life.

CHAPTER 7: FOOD

(Cultivating Inner Wellbeing)

"As is your food, so is your mind; as is your mind, so are your thoughts; as are your thoughts, so is your destiny."
— Upanishadic teaching, echoed in Ayurveda

You Are What You Think, Eat, And Absorb

"What you feed your mind and body, through food, water, and even the content you consume, shapes your reality."

Our overall well-being is influenced by what we consume—not solely through ingestion, but also via our visual, auditory, and cognitive inputs. From the materials we browse to the foods we consume, each input plays a role in shaping our brains through neuroplasticity and constructing our bodies—literally, on a cellular level.

Let me emphasize this so it becomes ingrained: what you feed your mind and body—through food, water, and even the content you consume—shapes your reality. This is not just philosophy; it's neuroscience, biochemistry, and ancient wisdom coming together in every cell of your being. Every 90 days, your cells completely renew—a direct reflection of your recent habits of consumption.

<u>You can have a completely new you at the Cellular level in just 90 days!</u>

Mental Consumption: Thoughts and Content Shape Your Reality

The old saying "you are what you think" carries more weight today than ever before. Just as food shapes our physical health, the content we consume—our thoughts, media, and daily inputs—shapes our inner world. In this digital age, our mental diet isn't just books and conversations. It's also the endless reels on Instagram, Snapchat, TikTok, or whatever platform we're plugged into. Without even realizing it, we often find ourselves comparing our raw, messy lives to the curated, filtered highlight reels of others. And this silent comparison can be toxic. It plants seeds of envy, inadequacy, and even obsession.

Recent research confirms something that many of us already know: upward social comparisons—seeing others seemingly living "better" lives—are closely associated with heightened levels of envy and symptoms of depression.

I have this idea that I like to think of as "The Neuroplasticity of Everyday Choices." Every thought, every morsel of food, every Instagram scroll, rewires your brain. Just think about that for a moment. Every decision you make, even the ones that might seem inconsequential, is helping to shape the structure of your brain.

And it's not just social comparisons that help warp and reshape our brains. Consider the kinds of headlines we're overwhelmed with: violent news, fear-driven media, and hyper-sexualized entertainment. These aren't neutral. For example, excess consumption of pornography results in overstimulation of the brain's reward circuitry, causing abnormally large amounts of dopamine to flood the brain. The brain then adapts, making those once-pleasurable experiences now feel like boredom, and we are left craving even more intense pleasures. Over time, this "supernormal stimulus" has the potential to create tolerance, compulsive use, and brain changes that resemble addiction. (More on that in the Chapter on Sex —I'll spare you the grim details there.)

The good news is that we can make conscious choices. And it begins with conscious decisions every minute along this journey. When we deliberately fill our minds with uplifting, soothing, or intellectually enriching materials, we create a new neural path in our minds. We become more focused, more empathetic, and more grounded. The brain responds to what we feed it, so why not feed it something we're enthusiastic about building on?

Ancient Wisdom: Sattva, Rajas, and Tamas

The Vedas classify foods and behaviors into three qualities:

- Sattva: Pure, harmonious, plant-based foods that promote clarity and peace.

- Rajas: Stimulating foods (spicy, salty, fried) that increase restlessness.

- Tamas: Heavy, processed, or stale foods that dull the mind and body.

Choosing sattvic foods—fresh, natural, and plant-based—aligns your body and mind with clarity and vitality.

The media we consume can be viewed through the same lens. Uplifting or educational content promotes a sattvic state of peace and understanding, while frantic, violent, or lust-inducing content introduces rajasic or tamasic qualities (restlessness or dullness) into our consciousness. Modern psychology supports this: practicing mindfulness, reading inspiring material, or engaging in creative, flow-based activities can all strengthen neural pathways associated with calmness and happiness. In contrast, doom-scrolling social media or bingeing on sensational content reinforces pathways of anxiety and craving.

When you consume information and experience a moment of epiphany, you create some of the most significant neural pathways, leading to a substantial release of dopamine, which is highly sustainable.

Assume command of your mental nourishment. Begin observing how your reading and viewing habits influence your mood and thoughts. Just as one would eliminate unhealthy food, consider reducing intake of "junk information." If social media provokes envy or loneliness, consider limiting its use or curating a feed composed of genuinely positive influences. If an excess of news induces anxiety, establish healthy boundaries. By intentionally "detoxing" your information consumption, you may discover that your typical mental state becomes more content and lucid. After all, a calm and focused mind fosters Creativity, Consciousness, and the capacity for reasoning, thereby generating both Human and Monetary Capital.

While the mind benefits from a nutritious intake of information, the body develops through the foods and beverages we consume. Consuming natural, whole foods contributes to a healthier physique. Conversely, consuming processed "junk" foods results in a "junk" body. Although this statement may seem direct, it reflects the reality. Scientific evidence has shown that our dietary choices have a direct impact on brain structure and function, ultimately affecting our mood and cognitive abilities.

Have you ever noticed how some people seem to carry an invisible presence—an energy that feels warm, grounded, and clear the moment they enter a room? It's not flashy or loud, but it's unmistakable. On the flip side, have you ever found yourself instinctively repelled by someone's vibe, their smell, or the air around them—without any apparent reason? As strange as it may sound, this phenomenon extends beyond physical appearance or personal hygiene.

The food we eat and the media we consume don't simply impact our physical condition and mental well-being; they subtly influence the essence and vibration we send out into the universe.

Every bite you taste and every perception you hold for even a short moment truly becomes a part of your being. The physical vessel is not a closed unit—instead, it absorbs, emanates, and conveys all that it takes in. If one consumes a wholesome diet of fish regularly, the breath and, subsequently, even the perspiration of an individual reveal shades of that peculiar fishy scent. Consume excessive quantities of pork, and an element of that aroma often remains attached. However, this is not only about physical scent—it's also about energetic residue. The food we eat carries its frequencies, and over time, those frequencies alter the essence of how we feel—and how others perceive us.

Eating as a Sacred Ritual: Hands, Grounding & Conscious Digestion

Digestion doesn't begin with your first bite. It starts the moment your senses perceive food—the vibrant colors, the inviting aromas, even the anticipation of flavors on your tongue. Your body, remarkably intuitive, immediately responds, secreting gastric juices tailored to precisely what you're about to consume.

Ever wondered why many traditional cultures insist on eating with their hands while seated cross-legged on the ground? You might think our ancestors ate with their hands simply because they had no utensils, but this overlooks a more profound truth: even royalty and nobility in ancient societies ate with their fingers. Kings and queens deliberately adopted this practice, not out of poverty, but due to profound wisdom.

When you eat with your hands, you create a direct sensory link with your food, conveying its texture, temperature, and energy to your brain. This tactile experience activates your nervous system, prompting your digestive organs to release specific digestive enzymes and gastric juices. Far from just tradition, eating with your hands actively supports digestion, leading to better nutrient absorption and smoother digestive processes.

Interestingly, many cultures around the world have traditions rooted in mindful eating. For example, in Japan, meals are often eaten family-style, sitting on the floor, using chopsticks, and free from digital distractions. This tradition, beyond its charming simplicity, encourages deep emotional bonds, conscious eating, and improved digestion.

Furthermore, sitting on the ground while eating isn't just a cultural practice—it's a way to stay energetically grounded. Ancient wisdom suggests that sitting on the floor creates a direct link with the Earth's energy. Eating in this grounded position helps balance your personal energy, allowing prana (vital energy) to flow more freely. Using your hands also helps ground the Earth's energy back into your body, promoting better digestion and overall health.

Contrast this with the modern habit of eating mindlessly—scrolling through smartphones, watching television, or multitasking. These distractions interfere with your brain's ability to signal the release of appropriate digestive enzymes, resulting in incomplete digestion. Such habits contribute to issues like indigestion, bloating, constipation, water retention, and, over time, more serious digestive disorders, including Crohn's Disease and Ulcerative Colitis. Ultimately, these chronic conditions are not just physical breakdowns but also deep disruptions of your gut microbiome and overall health.

A simple yet effective exercise you can try: sit on the floor with your family or loved ones, set aside digital distractions, and use your hands to eat your food slowly and mindfully. Feel the textures, enjoy the aromas, and fully engage with each bite. Notice how different this feels—how it grounds you, slows you down, and helps your body digest better. Watch how your mind clears, your body relaxes, and your digestion improves significantly.

Eating consciously isn't just about nutrition—it's about honoring the deep, sacred bond between your body, your food, and the Earth itself.

After all, you are what you eat, absorb, and consciously experience.

The 21/90 Rule: Crafting Habits, Building Lifestyles

It takes 21 days to create a habit,

It takes 90 days to create a lifestyle.

Ask: What one conscious habit will I commit to for 21 days?

Have you ever wondered why some changes seem to stick effortlessly while others fade just as quickly as they began? Science offers a surprisingly simple, yet powerful principle known as the 21/90 Rule. Here's how it works: if you commit to a new practice—whether it's meditation, journaling, walking, or mindful eating—for 21 consecutive days, it begins to form a habit.

That habit shifts into something you don't even have to think about; it starts to exist in your subconscious. But if you extend that same commitment to 90 days, it goes even further. It transforms from a habit into a lifestyle-a core part of who you are. Not just something you do, but someone you have become.

Energy Audit

You are always feeding yourself through food, water, words, and thoughts. Every choice is a vibration. Every habit has a frequency.

So pause and ask: "What am I nourishing in myself today?" Let your next choice be a conscious one.

CHAPTER 8: SLEEP

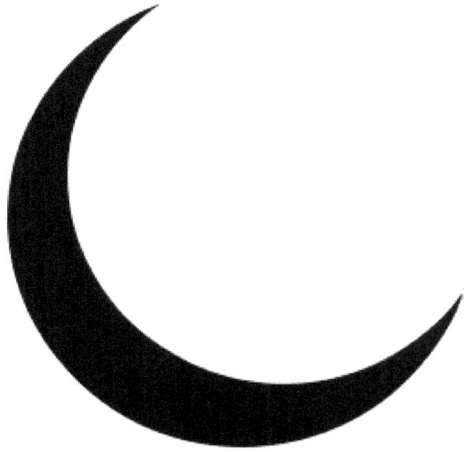

"Taking your energy higher in this lifetime," the ultimate goal matters because everything else—health, creativity, relationships, and success—**flows from it.**

"Taking your energy higher in this lifetime," the ultimate goal matters because everything else—health, creativity, relationships, and success—flows from it.

We previously discussed Breath, Nutrition, and ingestion (the first two pillars), and the Final Pillar is to prioritize sleep care.

When you align these three—sleep, breath, and nutrition—your energy multiplies, lifting you into clarity, resilience, and higher states of living.

Raising your energy isn't about chasing more; it's about aligning body, mind, and spirit so you can live, create, and contribute at your fullest potential.

Sleep - The Hidden Engine of Energy

The Sacred Role of Sleep

Sleep is not a pause button—it is one of the most profound regenerative processes of human life. While the body rests, the brain and nervous system remain active, reshaping connections, flushing toxins, balancing hormones, and laying down the foundations for learning, healing, and creativity.

Scientists now recognize what ancient traditions have always intuited: sleep is the hidden engine of energy.

What Really Happens When You Sleep

- **Heart rate slows; body heals.**

As you descend into deep sleep, your heart rate and blood pressure drop. This isn't just "rest"—it's a biological repair cycle. Your cardiovascular system undergoes a nightly reset, which helps reduce stress and inflammation.

- **Neuroplasticity in action.**

The brain rewires itself during sleep. Neural connections formed during the day are refined, strengthened, and pruned at night. This is why children—especially those under the age of seven- experience rapid brain development. Long hours of sleep allow their brains to form trillions of synaptic connections, laying the foundation for intelligence, empathy, and creativity.

- **The glymphatic cleanse.**

During sleep, the brain's glymphatic system flushes out waste proteins and toxins that accumulate during the day. Without this nightly cleansing, brain fog and fatigue pile up, leading to cognitive decline over time.

- **Dreams as integration.**

REM (Rapid Eye Movement) sleep is when memories and emotions are integrated into the deeper fabric of the mind. Dreams are not random—they are your subconscious reorganizing the files of the day, keeping what matters, discarding the rest.

The Sleep Deprivation Tragedy

Modern childhood sleep deprivation represents one of the most overlooked public health crises of our time. Adequate sleep during developmental stages is considered essential for normal brain development and plays a vital role in promoting healthy cognitive and psychosocial development.

When children don't get adequate sleep during critical periods:

- Neural pruning becomes impaired, leaving the brain cluttered with inefficient connections

- Emotional regulation centers develop poorly, leading to

increased anxiety and behavioral issues

- Memory consolidation suffers, making learning more difficult throughout life

- Growth hormone production decreases, affecting both physical and cognitive development

- The foundation for lifelong sleep patterns becomes disrupted

The tragedy is that these effects are largely irreversible. While the brain maintains some plasticity throughout life, the explosive growth opportunity of early childhood occurs only once.

The Adult Sleep Upgrade: Nightly System Optimization

While adult brains don't undergo the dramatic restructuring of childhood, sleep continues to provide profound benefits that most people dramatically underestimate.

The Neuroplastic Night Shift

Even in adulthood, your brain undergoes remarkable changes during sleep:

Memory Consolidation: During deep sleep, your brain replays the day's experiences up to 1,000 times faster than when they originally occurred. This high-speed replay transfers important information from temporary storage in the hippocampus to permanent storage in the cortex.

Skill Integration: Complex skills learned during the day—whether physical, cognitive, or creative—are integrated and improved during sleep. This is why you often wake up better at something than when you went to bed.

Creative Problem-Solving: REM sleep allows your brain to make novel connections between seemingly unrelated information, often leading to breakthrough insights and innovative solutions.

Emotional Processing: Sleep helps process emotional experiences, reducing their intensity while preserving their lessons. This is why "sleeping on" difficult decisions often leads to greater clarity.

Have you heard? Sleep and grow your muscles! Most Athletes, including Cristiano Ronaldo, have some very, very powerful sleep techniques…

People who consistently achieve deep, restorative sleep show:

- Lower resting heart rates during waking hours

- Better heart rate variability (a marker of cardiovascular health)

- Reduced risk of hypertension, heart disease, and stroke

- Improved athletic performance and recovery

Why Sleep Feels Like Rebirth: We know it intuitively: after a full, restorative night's sleep, we wake up with a mind that is sharper, a mood that is lighter, and a body that feels more alive. Add to that the profound joy of a clean, effortless bowel movement, and you touch an experience of alignment that rivals any peak pleasure.

That sensation—the freshness after deep sleep and full release—is one of life's simplest yet deepest joys. More renewing than indulgence, more grounding than fleeting excitement It is the daily chance to start again.

Sleep is not time lost to unconsciousness—it's time invested in conscious enhancement. Every night you prioritize quality sleep, you're making deposits in the bank account of your long-term health, cognitive capacity, and life satisfaction.

Sleep well. Your future self will thank you.

Energy Reboot: Sleep is not the end of your day. It's the beginning of your becoming. Each night, your body repairs, your mind rewires, your spirit realigns.

So before you close your eyes, ask: **"What energy do I want to rise with?"** Let your sleep be sacred. Let your awakening be powerful.

CHAPTER 9: GUT

Your Gut is your second Brain:
The Hidden Intelligence That Governs Your Life

"The gut is not simply a digestive organ—it is a second brain. Within its walls lies an intelligence that influences our moods, decisions, and even destiny."
— Michael D. Gershon, MD
(Author of The Second Brain)

The Gut-Brain Axis: Your Body's Internet

"The microbes in your gut are not just passengers—they are co-pilots of your consciousness."

The gut-brain axis is a bidirectional communication network that links the enteric and central nervous systems. This network is not only anatomical, but it also encompasses endocrine, humoral, metabolic, and immune routes of communication.

Think of your gut-brain axis as your body's private internet—a sophisticated communication network that never sleeps, never stops processing information, and constantly influences your experience of being alive.

This network operates through multiple communication channels:

The Vagus Nerve: Often referred to as the "information superhighway" between the gut and brain, this is the longest nerve in the body, directly connecting the enteric nervous system (the network of neurons in the gut) to the brainstem. It carries signals in both directions at incredible speeds.

Hormonal Pathways: Your gut produces over 20 different hormones, including many of the same ones found in your brain. These chemical messengers travel through your bloodstream, influencing everything from appetite to anxiety.

Immune Signaling: Approximately 70% of your immune system is located in your gut. Inflammatory signals from intestinal bacteria can trigger inflammatory responses in your brain, affecting mood and cognitive function.

Metabolic Messaging: The byproducts of bacterial digestion—called metabolites—serve as signaling molecules that can cross the blood-brain barrier and directly influence neural activity.

Neurotransmitter Production: Perhaps most remarkably, the bacteria in your gut actually produce many of the same neurotransmitters that govern your mental state.

This system is so sophisticated that scientists now refer to the gut as having its own "enteric nervous system"—containing over 500 million neurons, more than in the spinal cord. This network can function independently of the brain, making decisions about digestion, immune responses, and even mood regulation without conscious input.

You are not just a human being hosting 37 trillion cells. You are a walking ecosystem, home to over 100 trillion (total of 12 Zeros after 1!) microorganisms that collectively weigh about 2-3 pounds—roughly the same as your brain. These microbes don't just help you digest food; they manufacture neurotransmitters, influence your immune system, and constantly send signals that shape your thoughts, emotions, and behaviors.

The implications are staggering: your mood, your capacity for creativity, your ability to focus, your resilience under stress—all of these may be more influenced by the bacteria in your gut than by your genetics or your conscious choices.

Neurogastroenterology—the study of how our "second brain" in the gut communicates with and influences our first brain in ways that are revolutionizing our understanding of consciousness, mood, and human potential.

The Microbial Puppet Masters: How Bacteria Control Your Moods

Studies have reported on the biosynthesis of gut microbiome-derived neurotransmitters, including γ-aminobutyric acid (GABA), serotonin, dopamine, norepinephrine, and other neuroactive metabolites that could impact brain functions.

Your gut bacteria are not passive residents—they are active participants in your neurochemistry. Here's how specific microbes influence your mental states:

Serotonin: The Happiness Highway

More than 90% of the body's serotonin is synthesized in the gut by various bacteria, including Lactobacillus Reuteri, Bifidobacterium, and Escherichia. Contribute to serotonin production.

Serotonin is often referred to as the "happiness neurotransmitter," but that's an oversimplification. It's more like a master regulator of mood stability, impulse control, and emotional resilience.

When your gut bacteria aren't producing adequate serotonin, you might experience:

- Persistent low mood or depression

- Increased anxiety and worry

- Impulsive behavior and poor decision-making

- Sleep disturbances and irregular appetite

- Reduced capacity for joy and pleasure

The bacteria responsible for serotonin production thrive on specific nutrients:

Tryptophan (found in Beans, Potatoes, green peas, and pumpkin seeds), prebiotics (Fiber from vegetables and fruits), and fermented foods (Kimchi, Mommy's home-made pickles, and Sauerkraut) that introduce beneficial microbes directly.

GABA: The Natural Tranquilizer

Studies show that gut microbiota is capable of producing γ-aminobutyric acid (GABA), a key inhibitory neurotransmitter.

GABA is your brain's primary "brake pedal"—it calms neural activity and creates feelings of peace and relaxation. When gut bacteria produce adequate GABA, you experience:

- Natural stress resilience

- Better sleep quality

- Reduced anxiety and racing thoughts

- Improved focus and mental clarity

- Enhanced emotional regulation

Lactobacillus and Bifidobacterium strains are particularly effective GABA producers. These bacteria flourish when fed fermented foods, fiber-rich vegetables, and when stress levels are managed effectively.

The Modern Food Crisis: Thinning the Orchestra

Imagine walking through the Amazon rainforest—the overwhelming symphony of howler monkeys, woodpeckers, insects, and exotic birds forming a complex, beautiful cacophony evolved over millions of years. Now imagine that same forest paved into a concrete parking lot. The silence is deafening. A vibrant ecosystem has been replaced by sterile uniformity.

This is what we've done to our inner rainforest.

Our gut microbiome, once a full symphony of hundreds of microbial species working in harmony, has been reduced to a few scattered instruments struggling to hold a melody—causing havoc in our bodies and lives.

But this destruction didn't happen overnight.

Assault One: The Processed Food Invasion

Beginning in the 1950s, whole foods were replaced by engineered products built for shelf life, addictive taste, and profit—not health. Ultra-processed foods have become a primary source of calories, creating a gut environment that harms beneficial bacteria while promoting the growth of harmful ones.

- **The Sugar Tsunami:** Refined sugars and high-fructose corn syrup flood the gut, feeding pathogenic bacteria and yeasts that overpower beneficial species.

- **The Fiber Desert:** While ancestors consumed 50–100g of diverse fiber from many plants, modern diets average only 15g from limited sources. Without fiber, beneficial bacteria starve—especially those producing short-chain fatty acids vital for gut lining and brain signaling.

- **Chemical Warfare:** Ultra-processed foods contain thousands of additives (preservatives, emulsifiers, flavorings, colorants), many of which act as antimicrobials. They kill bacteria for shelf life, but also harm the essential bacteria in our gut.

Assault Two: The Pesticide Poisoning

Modern agriculture uses chemicals meant to kill living organisms, and they don't become harmless in our digestive system.

- **Glyphosate Devastation:** Glyphosate (Roundup), the world's most used herbicide, disrupts the shikimate pathway essential for bacterial amino acid production—starving beneficial bacteria.

- **Organophosphate Insecticides:** These disrupt insect nervous systems but also interfere with bacterial communication in the gut.

- **The Cocktail Effect:** We're exposed to mixtures of pesticides not tested together, creating amplified damage beyond individual effects.

Assault Three: The Antibiotic Apocalypse

Few forces have harmed our microbiomes more than excessive antibiotic use in medicine and agriculture.

- **Medical Overuse:** The average person receives 1–2 antibiotic courses per year, often for viral infections. Each course can reduce gut diversity by 25–50%, and some species never return.

- **Agricultural Contamination:** Around 80% of global antibiotics go to livestock—not for illness but to boost growth and prevent disease in overcrowded conditions. Antibiotic residues enter meat, dairy, and groundwater, causing continuous low-level microbiome disruption.

- **The Resistance Crisis:** Overuse has led to antibiotic-resistant bacteria ("superbugs") that thrive where beneficial bacteria cannot, producing toxins and inflammatory compounds that harm the intestinal lining.

But the damage extends beyond adults—it is now shaping microbiomes before life even begins.

The Sterile Generation: Children Born Into Microbial Poverty

Perhaps most concerning is what's happening to children born today. Many are entering the world with dramatically impoverished microbiomes due to:

C-Section Delivery: Babies born via caesarean section miss the first crucial microbial inoculation that occurs during vaginal birth.

Formula Feeding: Breast milk contains specific sugars (oligosaccharides) that feed beneficial bacteria. Formula-fed babies develop different, less diverse microbiomes.

Early Antibiotic Exposure: Children now receive an average of 3-4 courses of antibiotics before age 2, during the critical window when their microbiomes are establishing.

Hygiene Hypothesis Reality: While basic hygiene prevents disease, excessive sanitization prevents children from acquiring the environmental microbes they need for immune system development and microbial diversity.

Processed Food from Birth: Many children consume ultra-processed foods as primary nutrition sources from weaning, never establishing robust bacterial communities.

From Rainforest to Parking Lot: The Numbers

The microbial devastation is measurable and shocking:

- Hunter-gatherer populations maintain 150-200 distinct bacterial species in their guts

- Rural populations in developing countries average 100-120 species

- Urban Americans average 40-60 species, with many people harboring fewer than 30

The Anxiety-Microbiome Feedback Loop

When gut bacteria are imbalanced, they can lead to chronic, low-grade inflammation that activates your stress response system. This creates what researchers call "neuroinflammation"—inflammatory signaling in the brain that can persist for months or years.

"Notice how you panic even though everything is just fine, your brain conjures up scenarios that never play out."

Neuroinflammation literally changes how you process information:

- **Threat Detection Hypersensitivity**: You perceive neutral situations as dangerous

- **Negative Cognitive Bias**: You automatically focus on potential problems rather than opportunities

- **Reduced Cognitive Flexibility**: You have difficulty seeing alternative perspectives or solutions

- **Impaired Decision-Making**: You make choices based on fear rather than wisdom

The Creativity-Gut Connection

Emerging research suggests that gut bacteria influence creativity and innovation capacity. Certain bacterial strains produce metabolites that enhance neuroplasticity—your brain's ability to form new neural connections and think in novel ways.

When your gut microbiome is diverse and balanced:

- **Enhanced Pattern Recognition**: You notice connections others miss

- **Increased Openness to Experience**: You're more willing to try new approaches

- **Improved Flow States**: You enter deep focus more easily

- **Greater Cognitive Flexibility**: You can switch between different thinking styles

Anyway, the list of problems keeps going on and on… but my **GUT** tells me you are ready for a solution and want to restore!

The Restoration Protocol: Rebuilding Your Second Brain

Understanding the problem is the first step. The second step is taking conscious action to restore your gut-brain axis to optimal function. This isn't just about probiotics—it's about creating an integrated system that supports the bacteria-brain partnership.

Phase 1: Remove the Toxins (Weeks 1-2)

Before adding beneficial bacteria, you must stop poisoning them:

Eliminate Ultra-Processed Foods: Remove foods with more than 5 ingredients or any ingredients you can't pronounce. This immediately reduces your intake of gut-damaging chemicals.

Cut Refined Sugars: Refined sugar feeds harmful bacteria while starving beneficial ones. Replace with fruits, vegetables, and natural sweeteners in moderation.

Completely Avoid any Animal Products: Since we are no longer Hunter-Gatherers, we definitely don't know what we caught and where, and what was put into them or injected into them for them to make it to our tables!

Filter Your Water: Chlorine in tap water acts as an antimicrobial. Use a quality carbon filter to remove chlorine while retaining beneficial minerals.

Phase 2: Feed the Beneficial Bacteria (Weeks 2-4)

Diverse Fiber Sources: Aim for 30+ grams daily from a variety of sources, including vegetables, fruits, nuts, seeds, and properly prepared grains and legumes.

Prebiotic Foods: artichokes, onions, garlic, leeks, asparagus, and green bananas contain specific fibers that beneficial bacteria thrive on.

Resistant Starch: Cooked and cooled potatoes, rice, and oats create resistant starch that feeds beneficial bacteria in your colon.

Polyphenol-Rich Foods: Berries, dark chocolate, green tea, and colorful vegetables provide compounds that beneficial bacteria convert into neurotransmitter precursors.

Phase 3: Introduce Beneficial Microbes (Weeks 3-6)

Fermented Foods: Kefir, yogurt, sauerkraut, kimchi, miso, and kombucha introduce live beneficial bacteria. Aim for 1-2 servings daily.

Targeted Probiotics: Choose strains based on specific goals:

- **Lactobacillus helveticus** and **Bifidobacterium longum** for anxiety reduction

- **Lactobacillus plantarum** for cognitive enhancement

- **Lactobacillus casei** for mood stability

- **Lactobacillus reuteri** for enhanced skin, thicker hair, and most importantly, releasing more serotonin

- **Bifidobacterium infantis** for overall gut-brain axis support

Soil-Based Organisms: Bacillus species and other soil-based probiotics help establish microbial diversity that modern hygiene practices have eliminated.

Playing in the mud with your kids may be great for you 😊

Phase 4: Support the Ecosystem (Ongoing)
Circadian Rhythm Optimization: Your gut bacteria have their own daily rhythms. Regular sleep-wake cycles support bacterial health and the production of neurotransmitters.

Stress Management: Chronic stress directly damages beneficial bacteria. Daily meditation, yoga, or other stress-reduction practices are essential.

Regular Movement: Exercise increases beneficial bacterial diversity and enhances the production of mood-boosting metabolites.

Social Connection: Believe it or not, isolation changes gut bacteria composition. Regular meaningful social interactions support both mental health and microbial diversity.

The Long Game

Rebuilding a healthy gut-brain axis is not a quick fix—it's a lifestyle transformation. Significant changes typically occur within 4-12 weeks, but optimal function may take 6-12 months or longer, especially if you're recovering from years of gut damage.

The investment is worth it. When your gut-brain axis functions optimally, you experience life from a fundamentally different state of consciousness—more resilient, creative, emotionally balanced, and intuitively connected to your environment and relationships.

Fix your inner self, and the outer world will fix itself! - Core of any human transformation!

Every problem in life is first an inner misalignment — of emotion, belief, or focus.

The moment your inner code is debugged, the outer system begins to self-heal.

Small Note: *As you may already know, I am not a medical doctor, so I am unable to offer any further insight, as this is a current area of deeper research for me.*

I have benefited from using these techniques, and I humbly offer them to you. 😊

CHAPTER 10: HAPPINESS

Joy is Your Competitive Advantage

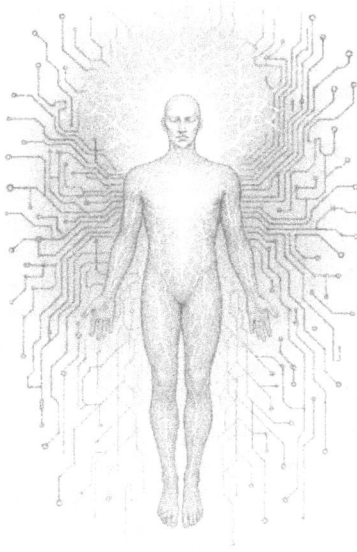

"Happiness is not something ready-made. It comes
from your own actions."
— Dalai Lama

Dr. Sarah Patel stood before her neuroscience team, holding two brain scans. One glowed with vibrant neural activity—networks firing in harmonious patterns, neurotransmitters flowing like rivers of light. The other showed minimal activation, sparse connections, and areas of relative darkness.

"Same person," she announced. "Same brain. Twelve weeks apart."

The room fell silent. These weren't scans from someone recovering from trauma or starting antidepressants. They were from a participant in their consciousness study—someone who had learned to operate from what the research team had begun calling "authentic happiness" rather than its counterfeit alternatives.

"What changed?" a researcher asked.

Dr. Patel smiled. "They stopped seeking happiness outside themselves and started generating it from within. They learned the difference between <u>pleasure and joy</u>, between <u>external validation and internal fulfillment</u>. Most importantly, they discovered that happiness isn't something that happens to you—it's something you create through how you engage with life."

Happiness isn't just a feeling—it's a measurable, reproducible state of optimal brain function that can be cultivated through conscious practice.

Internal vs. External Happiness: The Fundamental Distinction

"Happiness is not a destination you reach—it's an operating system you run."

The modern capitalist industry has repeatedly sold us a lie: that joy comes from accumulating experiences, possessions, or achievements that are external to ourselves. This external approach creates what researchers call "hedonic adaptation"—the frustrating phenomenon in which each new pleasure provides only temporary satisfaction before we return to baseline, requiring ever-greater stimulation to feel good.

External happiness operates like an addiction cycle:

- Initial euphoria from a new acquisition or experience

- Gradual return to normal mood levels

- Increased craving for the next "hit"

- Escalating requirements for the same satisfaction

- Underlying emptiness that never quite gets filled

Internal happiness functions entirely differently. It emerges from alignment between your actions and values, from contributing meaningfully to something beyond yourself, from the neurochemical rewards of growth, connection, and purpose.

The neuroscience is clear: brains operating from internal happiness show enhanced connectivity between regions associated with creativity, empathy, and higher-order thinking. They produce optimal levels of serotonin, dopamine, and other neurotransmitters without requiring external triggers.

The Eight-Word Operating System

Michael Anthony's research revealed something profound: human happiness can be distilled into eight words that function as an internal compass:

"I am always truthful, positive, and helping others."

This isn't naive optimism or moral preaching; it's practical neuroscience. When you align your behavior with these principles, your brain literally functions better:

Truthfulness eliminates the cognitive load of maintaining false narratives. Your brain doesn't have to track lies, manage contradictory information, or deal with the stress of potential exposure. The energy freed up becomes available for creativity and higher-order thinking.

Positivity (genuine, not forced) optimizes your neurochemistry for problem-solving and opportunity recognition. Positive emotions broaden your cognitive scope, helping you notice possibilities that stress and negativity obscure.

Helping others activates reward centers in your brain more sustainably than self-focused activities. Neuroscientists refer to this as "helper's high"—the neurochemical reward system that evolved to encourage cooperation and community building.

The Physiology of Joy

Happiness isn't confined to your brain—it's a whole-body experience with measurable physical effects:

Cardiovascular System: Happy people show improved heart rate variability, lower blood pressure, and reduced risk of heart disease.

Immune Function: Positive emotions strengthen immune responses, improving resistance to illness and faster recovery times.

Digestive Health: Stress and negative emotions disrupt gut bacteria and digestive function, while happiness promotes optimal digestion and nutrient absorption.

Sleep Quality: Internal happiness is associated with deeper, more restorative sleep patterns and a faster sleep onset.

Longevity: Multiple studies have shown that happy people live longer, with some research suggesting a 7-10-year increase in lifespan.

Transforming Emotional Patterns

The key to sustainable happiness lies not in avoiding negative emotions but in transforming your relationship with them. Instead of suppressing complicated feelings, you can learn to:

Recognize Patterns: Notice when you're operating from fear, anger, or scarcity rather than love, curiosity, or abundance.

Separate Facts from Emotions: Understanding that events are neutral and your emotional responses are choices you make based on interpretation.

Reframe Circumstances: Ask "How might this situation serve my growth?" rather than "Why is this happening to me?"

Focus on Process over Outcome: Find satisfaction in your effort and growth rather than only in external results.

"Our brains are capable of creating every scenario that will never occur in Reality." – The Overthinker

This isn't about becoming emotionally numb—it's about developing emotional mastery where your responses serve your wellbeing rather than undermining it.

The Practice of Sustainable Happiness

Building authentic happiness requires consistent practice, similar to developing physical fitness:

Morning Intention Setting: Begin each day by consciously choosing your emotional and mental state rather than letting circumstances dictate your experience.

Gratitude Practice: Regularly acknowledge what's working in your life, training your brain to notice positive aspects of your experience. If you are in good health, you already know what to be most grateful for.

Service Orientation: Regularly engage in activities that benefit others, triggering the neurochemical rewards of contribution and connection.

Truthfulness: Eliminate lies (including small ones) from your communication to reduce cognitive load and increase self-respect.

Present-Moment Awareness: Practice returning your attention to the present moment, rather than being lost in regrets about the past or anxious about the future.

Emotional Regulation: Develop the skill of choosing your responses to circumstances rather than reacting automatically from old patterns.

Joy Signal

Happiness isn't a reward. It's a rhythm. A signal your body sends when your soul is aligned.

So, before you chase the next achievement, pause.

Ask yourself: **"Am I generating joy—or outsourcing it?"**

Let your truth be your compass. Let your joy be your signal. Let your life become the transmission.

CHAPTER 11: MONEY

Money as Energy - Transforming Your Financial Relationship

When Money Becomes Your Ally, Not Your Master

"Money is amplified energy. Increase your energy,
and money flows more readily toward you."

Money, at its essence, is a medium of energy exchange. It represents stored human effort, creativity, and value creation. Understanding this fundamental nature changes how you relate to it.

"By no means am I suggesting that one should not earn a lot of Money, drop their ambitions, create consciousness and awareness, and become a saint, turning away from their responsibilities to themselves and their families.

What I am suggesting is to become conscious and increase your energy to the point where you have an unending flow of Money in your life.

Also, each one of us, even the richest amongst us, needs to improve their relationship with Money." Consider this a continuous and ongoing process.

The Energy-Money Connection

When you're operating from high-energy states, several things happen that improve your financial outcomes:

Enhanced Decision-Making: High energy correlates with better cognitive function, leading to clearer thinking about financial choices, investment opportunities, and career decisions.

Increased Productivity: Energy directly translates to output. When you can accomplish more in less time while maintaining quality, your economic value increases.

Improved Creativity: Financial success often requires creative problem-solving, whether in business, investing, or career advancement. Creativity flourishes when energy is abundant.

Stronger Relationships: Most financial opportunities arise from strong relationships. High-energy people are more attractive as partners, collaborators, and investment targets.

Risk Assessment: Optimal energy levels improve your ability to assess risks accurately—neither being overly cautious due to fear nor recklessly aggressive due to desperation.

The Abundance-Scarcity Energy Shift

Abundance Practices:

- Focus on opportunities rather than limitations

- Celebrate others' success rather than feeling threatened

- Invest in experiences and capabilities that enhance energy

- Practice gratitude for current resources while working toward goals

If I were a betting Man, I would say we are all going to make it and achieve all our dreams, fulfill all our wishes, and take care of our families. 😊

The leaders unveiling the AI technology of our Time are also those calling for an abundantly prosperous and wealthy future for all humanity.

Scarcity Warning Signs:

- Constant worry about money despite adequate resources

- Reluctance to invest in yourself or others

- Viewing money as something to hoard rather than circulate

- Feeling threatened by others' financial success

Money Working for You: The Energy of Financial Independence

The goal isn't just accumulating money but creating systems that generate energy rather than consume it.

Passive Income as Energy Liberation

Investment Income: Returns from well-chosen investments provide income without requiring time spent trading, thereby preserving energy for higher-value activities.

Business Systems: Businesses that operate without constant personal input free up energy for strategic thinking and new opportunities.

Intellectual Property: Creating assets that generate ongoing returns (such as books, courses, patents, and royalties) leverages past energy into future income.

Real Estate: Property investments that appreciate and generate rental income can provide passive cash flow.

The Energy Compound Effect

As financial systems begin working for you rather than you working for them, energy compounds:

Time Liberation: Spending less time on financial survival creates space for creative and strategic thinking.

Stress Reduction: Financial security helps reduce cortisol levels and enhances cognitive capacity, leading to better decision-making.

Opportunity Recognition: When not focused on immediate financial needs, you can recognize longer-term opportunities others miss.

Risk Capacity: Financial cushions allow for strategic risks that can accelerate growth.

"We have enough examples of the Super–Wealthy who just transform and buy Health and Time in their lives as they spend their money to increase their physical abundance."

"A prime example is of a guy who spent his early life building companies and then at 45 sold his company for $100 million, and now his only goal is to reverse Aging. To the tune of calling aging a disease and holding his motto – Don't Die"

- I am talking of Bryan Johnson, who turned all his Biomarkers to be 20-something again ☺ He made news for spending $2 million a year on becoming younger….

Mahalakshmi: Money as Divine Abundance

In Vedantic tradition, money in its purest form represents Devi Mahalakshmi—the goddess of wealth, prosperity, and abundance. This isn't about worshipping money as a deity but rather understanding wealth as a manifestation of cosmic intelligence and natural flow.

Mahalakshmi represents abundance that serves dharma (righteous purpose). Unlike mere accumulation or hoarding, Lakshmi-aligned wealth flows where it can create the greatest good. The ancient texts describe her as dwelling in a place of cleanliness, order, generosity, and devotion to higher purposes.

To see money as *Mahalakshmi* is to shift from **possession to participation**, from **accumulation to alignment**. This is the perspective that transforms how we relate to money:

Money is not a master to serve, nor a trophy to chase. It is energy — a reflection of your inner state, a measure of the value you create, and the consciousness with which you circulate it.

When you hold this view, the pursuit of wealth becomes sacred. You begin to realize that **how you earn, spend, and give** determines not just your financial balance, but your energetic one.

- **Earning** becomes a creative expression of service.

- **Spending** becomes an act of nourishment — supporting life, beauty, and purpose.

- **Saving and investing** become acts of stewardship — planting seeds that sustain future growth.

- **Giving** becomes the purest circulation of energy — dissolving ego and expanding flow.

True prosperity, then, is not measured in possessions but in **peace**, **freedom**, and **flow**.

The Flow Principle

Energy that is hoarded stagnates; energy that flows multiplies. Just as oxygen sustains life by movement, money sustains value by circulation.

When your energy is high and your intention pure, abundance naturally finds you — through ideas, people, and opportunities. The key is to keep energy moving, aligned with gratitude, generosity, and a growth mindset.

"Wealth that flows serves the world. Wealth that stops, decays."

The Real Goal: Energy Sovereignty

Financial independence is not just about never worrying about money — it's about never letting money control your energy. You reach a state where your finances sustain your freedom, your freedom fuels your creativity, and your creativity keeps the energy in motion.

At this stage, **money becomes your ally** — not as currency, but as *current*.
It moves through you, amplifying everything you touch with awareness.

"When consciousness leads and currency follows, abundance becomes inevitable."

"To honor Mahalakshmi is to live in rhythm with the cosmic flow — creating, giving, and receiving with grace. In that flow, abundance ceases to be a goal and becomes your natural state of being."

CHAPTER 12: CURRENCY

The Currency of Consciousness Is Meaning

"The mystery of human existence lies not in just
staying alive, but in finding something to live for."
— Fyodor Dostoevsky

Meaning is the New Motivation

The boardroom was silent except for the soft hum of the air conditioning. Twelve executives sat around a mahogany table worth more than most people's homes, staring at charts that painted a picture of unprecedented success. Revenue was up 240% from the previous year. Stock prices had tripled. By every conventional metric, they had won.

Yet Julie Chen, the CEO who had built this empire from a tiny startup in her garage, felt hollow.

"We've achieved everything we set out to do," she announced, her voice steady but distant. "And I've never felt emptier. – This was the true voice within her."

This wasn't supposed to happen. Success was supposed to feel... successful. But somewhere between the IPO celebrations and the magazine covers declaring her "Entrepreneur of the Year," Julie had lost something she couldn't quite name. The fire that once drove her to work eighteen-hour days had dimmed to barely glowing embers.

She wasn't alone. Across Silicon Valley, Wall Street, and corporate towers worldwide, a quiet revolution has begun. The most successful people on the planet are asking a question that would have seemed absurd to previous generations:

What's the point of winning if the game itself feels meaningless?

The Great Awakening in Corner Offices

Something unprecedented is happening in the upper echelons of business and entrepreneurship. CEOs who have achieved everything money can buy are stepping away from the traditional playbook of endless growth and profit maximization. They're asking more profound questions about purpose, impact, and what it truly means to build something worthwhile.

- The rise of "purpose-driven CEOs" as documented: one study found more than 25% of CEOs already identify as purpose-driven, and 59% are in the process of developing a purpose statement.

This shift isn't coming from external pressure or market forces. It's emerging from an internal recognition that the old metrics of success—revenue, market share, valuations—while necessary, don't address the human need for meaning and fulfilment. The most driven achievers discover that their success feels surprisingly empty when it lacks deeper purpose.

Consider Marc Benioff of Salesforce, who has transformed his company's mission from simply selling software to creating positive social change. Or Yvon Chouinard, who gave away his billion-dollar Patagonia Company to fight climate change, declaring, "Earth is now our only shareholder." These aren't isolated cases of wealthy eccentrics; they represent a fundamental shift in how the most successful people think about success itself.

The neuroscience behind this transformation is fascinating. When we achieve goals driven purely by external validation—such as money, status, or recognition—our brains experience a brief dopamine spike, followed by a need for more dopamine, which does not materialize with more money, status, or even fame. We quickly return to baseline happiness levels, often feeling even more empty than before. But when our achievements align with deeper values and contribute to something beyond ourselves, we tap into more sustainable sources of fulfilment.

This is why meaning has become the new motivation. It's not that money doesn't matter—it's that money without meaning creates a special kind of suffering that no amount of wealth can cure.

Conscious Growth vs. Chaotic Scale: Redefining Success

The old model of business growth was simple: bigger is always better. More customers, more revenue, more market share, more everything.

Scale at all costs. Move fast and break things. Growth for growth's sake became the unquestioned gospel of the business world.

But this approach, what we might call "chaotic scale," often leads to organizations that are large but fragile, profitable but purposeless, successful but soulless. Companies grow so fast that they lose touch with their original mission. They become machines optimized for extraction rather than creation, taking value from the world rather than adding it.

Conscious growth operates from a different paradigm. It asks not just "How can we grow?" but "How should we grow? What kind of growth serves not just our shareholders but all stakeholders? What does sustainable, meaningful expansion look like?"

Consider the difference between Amazon's relentless expansion into every conceivable market and Patagonia's deliberate restraint, which encourages customers to buy less while building a more sustainable business model. Both are successful, but they represent fundamentally different philosophies of growth.

Chip Bergh, CEO of Levi Strauss & Co., emphasized that company values are "key to longevity" in an era where consumers expect alignment of purpose and brand.

Conscious growth recognizes that:

- **Quality matters more than quantity.** A smaller customer base that truly loves what you do is more valuable than a massive audience that's merely indifferent.

- **Sustainability trumps speed.** Building something that lasts for decades requires different choices than creating something that lasts only briefly.

- **Purpose drives performance.** Teams aligned around meaningful missions consistently outperform those motivated solely by financial incentives.

- **Stakeholder value beats shareholder value.** Companies that serve employees, customers, communities, and the environment alongside shareholders tend to outperform those focused solely on stock prices.

This doesn't mean abandoning ambition or accepting mediocrity. Conscious growth can be incredibly ambitious; it's just ambitious about different things. It seeks to optimize human flourishing, environmental regeneration, and societal benefit alongside financial returns.

The most interesting finding from neuroscience research is that leaders who shift from chaotic scale to conscious growth don't just feel better about their work; they often perform better, too. Purpose-driven motivation tends to be more resilient, sustainable, and creative than motivation driven by fear or greed.

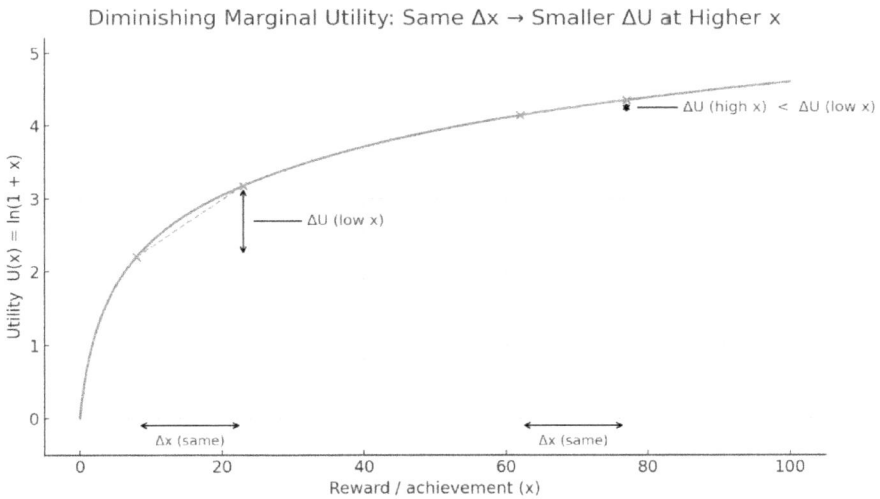

Diminishing Marginal Utility: Same Δx → Smaller ΔU at Higher x

Why Meaning Matters More than any Currency

"The brands that will thrive in the coming years are the ones that have a purpose beyond profit," Richard Branson has said — a succinct framing for why meaning now sits at the heart of modern success narratives. But this isn't just a business principle; it's a profoundly human one.

Viktor Frankl, a Holocaust survivor and psychiatrist, spent his life studying what makes existence worthwhile. His conclusion was radical in its simplicity: "Everything can be taken from a man but one thing: the last of the human freedoms—to choose one's attitude in any given set of circumstances, to choose one's own way."

Frankl discovered that humans can endure almost any suffering if they can find meaning in it, but even the most comfortable circumstances become unbearable without purpose. This insight has profound implications for how we think about work, success, and wealth.

Modern neuroscience validates Frankl's observations. When we engage in meaningful activities that align with our values, relationships that matter, contributions that make a difference, our brains release a cocktail of neurochemicals associated with well-being: serotonin, oxytocin, endorphins, and dopamine. This neurochemical signature is entirely different from the fleeting satisfaction we derive from materialistic achievements.

More fascinating still, meaning doesn't just feel better—it literally rewires our brains for resilience, creativity, and sustained high performance. People who report high levels of meaning in their work show:

- **Enhanced cognitive flexibility** - they're better at solving complex problems and adapting to change

- **Improved stress resilience** - they bounce back faster from setbacks and maintain equilibrium under pressure

- **Increased creativity** - they generate more innovative solutions and think more expansively

- **Greater persistence** - they stick with challenging tasks longer and recover more quickly from failure

This is why the most successful entrepreneurs and leaders are increasingly optimizing for meaning alongside profit. They've discovered that meaning isn't the opposite of success—it's the sustainable foundation of authentic success.

Money, by contrast, is a poor primary motivator. Beyond meeting basic needs, additional wealth shows diminishing returns on happiness. The billionaire isn't necessarily happier than the millionaire, who isn't necessarily happier than someone making $75,000 a year. But the person

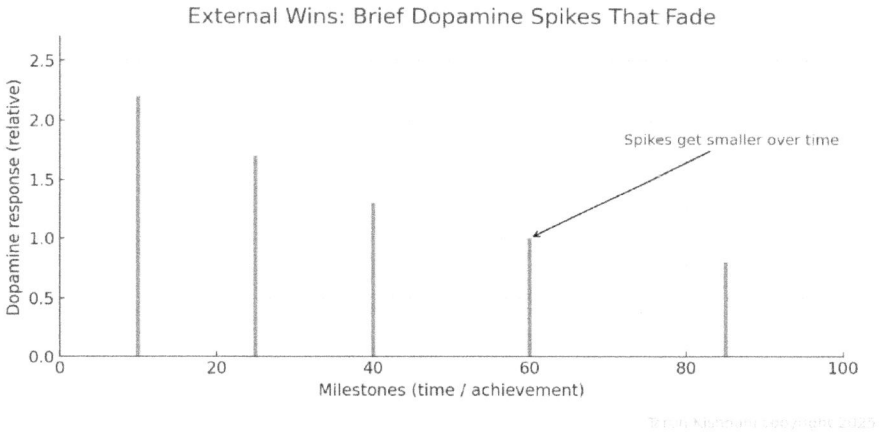

External Wins: Brief Dopamine Spikes That Fade

Spikes get smaller over time

whose work contributes to something they deeply care about—regardless of their income level—consistently reports higher levels of life satisfaction.

This doesn't mean money is unimportant. Financial security provides freedom, options, and the ability to contribute more significantly. But money works best as a byproduct of meaningful work rather than its primary purpose.

The Neuroscience of Purpose

Your brain is literally designed for meaning-making. The human nervous system evolved not just to survive, but to find patterns, create narratives, and locate purpose within experience. When we can connect our daily actions to a larger story—about who we are, why we matter, and how we contribute—we activate neural networks associated with motivation, resilience, and well-being.

Researchers have identified a specific brain network called the "default mode network" that becomes active during rest and introspection. When this network is functioning optimally, it helps integrate experiences into coherent narratives about identity and purpose. People with a strong sense of meaning show more coherent activity in this network.

Conversely, when work feels meaningless—when we can't connect our efforts to anything we care about—different neural patterns emerge. The brain treats meaningless work similarly to how it processes threats, activating stress response systems and depleting cognitive resources. This is why jobs that are well-paid but purposeless often lead to burnout, depression, and a variety of stress-related health issues.

The implications for business and career choices are profound. Organizations that help employees connect their work to meaningful outcomes don't just have happier workers—they have workers whose brains are literally optimized for better performance.

Rewriting the Success Script

The traditional script for success goes something like this: work hard, make money, accumulate status symbols, retire comfortably, and hope you'll figure out what makes you happy along the way. This script worked reasonably well in an era of scarcity, when financial security was the primary challenge most people faced.

But we're living in an era of unprecedented abundance. More people than ever before in human history have access to education, technology, and opportunities. The primary challenge isn't survival—it's significance. It's not "How do I make enough money?" but "How do I make my life matter?"

The new script for success looks different:

1. **Start with why.** Before asking "What can I do to make money?" ask "What problems do I feel called to solve? What kind of world do I want to help create?"

2. **Build skills that serve the mission.** Develop capabilities not just because they're marketable, but because they enable you to contribute more meaningfully to causes you care about.

3. **Measure progress holistically.** Track not just financial metrics but also impact metrics: lives touched, problems solved, positive changes catalyzed.

4. **Optimize for sustainable satisfaction.** Make choices that you'll still feel good about in ten years, not just choices that maximize short-term gains.

5. **Create value, don't just capture it.** Focus on adding something meaningful to the world rather than simply extracting profit from existing systems.

This doesn't mean abandoning practical considerations or accepting poverty in the name of purpose. The most sustainable approach integrates meaning and money, purpose and profit, contribution and compensation. But it starts with the deeper questions and lets the financial success flow from genuine value creation.

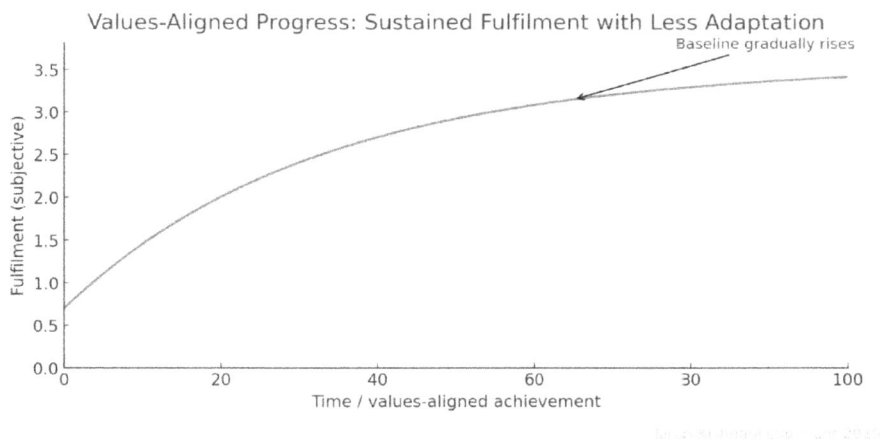

Values-Aligned Progress: Sustained Fulfilment with Less Adaptation

The depth of your peace measures real wealth.

Every choice you make to prioritize meaning alongside money, to choose conscious growth over chaotic scale, rewires your brain for greater fulfillment and sustainable success. This isn't just feel-good philosophy—it's a practical strategy for building a life and career that remain satisfying across decades rather than burning out in years.

The question isn't whether you can afford to prioritize meaning. The question is whether you can afford not to. In a world where meaningless work increasingly feels like a form of slow spiritual death, choosing purpose might be the most practical decision you ever make.

This is where I personally think AI can be a great benefactor and level player, helping us augment tedious, repetitive tasks, freeing up a lot of our time to reach the heights of our creativity!

Your brain is designed for meaning. Your life is designed for contribution. Your work can be designed to honor both while still creating the financial abundance that supports your freedom and impact.

The currency of consciousness isn't measured in dollars—it's measured in the depth of your peace, the quality of your contributions, and the alignment between who you are and what you do. This is the new wealth. This is where real success lives.

Meaning Check

You've chased success. You've felt the shift.

Now ask yourself: Am **I making money… or making meaning?**

CHAPTER 13: CREATIVITY

The Last Frontier of Human Supremacy

"Creativity is just connecting things." — Steve Jobs

The notification chimed at 3:47 AM on a cold Winter Morning in December 2023 (Sora – Video AI Generator had dropped the night before), jolting Sandy awake. Her phone screen glowed with an urgent message from her creative director: "The AI just generated 500 logo variations in twelve minutes. Same brief that took our team three weeks. We need to talk."

Sandy Miller is the Founder of Digital Ad Agency, which works with Fortune 100 companies. She started it from her dorm in Parsons New School of Design, but today lives in a penthouse in Chelsea. As the founder of one of NYC's most prestigious creative agencies, she'd built her reputation on the irreplaceable value of human imagination. Now, watching artificial intelligence create stunning visuals, write compelling copy, and even compose music, she wondered: What's left for humans to create?

The answer came to her not through logic, but through a memory—a moment of pure creative breakthrough that had defined her career. It was ten years ago, during the pitch for their biggest client. The presentation was failing. Charts and data weren't connecting. The room felt cold, corporate, and lifeless.

Then Sandy did something unexpected. She threw away her script and told a story about her grandmother's hands—weathered from years of sewing, but capable of creating the most beautiful quilts she had ever seen. She spoke about how those hands had taught her that creativity wasn't just about making things; it was about weaving love, memory, and meaning into every stitch.

The room was transformed. Executives leaned forward. One person quietly wiped away a tear. They won the account not because of a superior strategy or clever wordplay. Still, because Sandy had done something no algorithm could replicate, she had felt something deeply and shared that feeling with others.

This is the code of creativity that AI cannot crack—the uniquely human ability to create from emotion, to transform feelings into form, and to evoke emotions in others, which is deeply, deeply ingrained in human nature.

"People don't buy what you do; they buy why you do it." — Simon Sinek, American Author and Motivational Speaker.

Let me explain this differently so that I can drive the point home

Emotion over Logic: The Human Advantage

While artificial intelligence excels at pattern recognition, optimization, and logical processing, it fundamentally lacks the emotional depth that drives truly transformative creativity. AI can analyze millions of successful advertisements and generate variations, but it cannot feel the heartbreak that inspires a song or the righteous anger that fuels social change.

The pain of loss, the ecstasy of love, the frustration of injustice, the wonder of discovery—these emotional states become the raw materials for creation.

Neuroscience reveals why emotion is so crucial to creativity. The brain's emotional centers (particularly the limbic system) are deeply interconnected with areas responsible for memory, meaning-making, and creative synthesis. When we create from an emotional place, we activate neural networks that pure logic cannot access.

Consider the difference between AI-generated music and a song written by someone processing grief. The AI might produce technically proficient melodies that follow successful patterns, but the human-created song carries something irreplaceable—the resonance of lived experience. It connects with listeners not just through sound, but through the shared humanity of having a heart.

This emotional foundation gives human creativity several unique advantages:

Authenticity: Our creations carry the signature of our experiences. They reflect not just what we think, but who we are and what we've lived through.

Resonance: Since our creativity stems from universal human emotions, it can resonate with others in profound ways. We create not just for ourselves, but from our shared humanity.

Evolution: Our emotional experiences are constantly changing, which means our creative expression evolves too. Each heartbreak, triumph, or moment of wonder adds new colors to our creative palette.

Purpose: Human creativity often carries intention beyond mere aesthetics—to heal, to protest, to celebrate, to make sense of existence itself.

Jensen Huang (CEO of NVIDIA): His leadership emphasizes the leveraging of creativity and technology. He says, "Innovation is not about inventing something new — it's about improving what already exists."

The Neurochemistry of Creative Flow

When humans create a place of emotional authenticity, something remarkable happens in the brain. We enter what psychologist Mihaly Csikszentmihalyi calls "flow state"—a condition of effortless concentration and peak performance.

During creative flow, the brain releases a cocktail of neurochemicals that enhance both performance and satisfaction:

- **Dopamine** heightens focus and pattern recognition

- **Norepinephrine** increases attention and emotional intensity

- **Endorphins** create pleasure and reduce the perception of effort

- **Anandamide** promotes lateral thinking, novel connections leading to a state of bliss.

- **Serotonin** enhances mood and social connection

This neurochemical symphony cannot be artificially induced through logic alone—it emerges from the interplay between emotional engagement and creative expression. This is why artists often describe their best work as coming "through them" rather than "from them."

AI processes information, but humans transform information through the alchemy of emotion, creating something entirely new in the process.

The Joy-Creativity Loop

Joy and creativity reinforce each other in a positive feedback loop:

1. **Joy opens perception:** When we feel good, we notice more possibilities and connections

2. **Joy reduces fear:** Creative risk-taking becomes easier when we're not operating from anxiety

3. **Joy enhances playfulness:** The spirit of play is essential for creative experimentation

4. **Creation amplifies joy:** The act of creating something meaningful increases our happiness

5. **Shared joy builds community:** When our creations bring others joy, it deepens our own satisfaction

This loop explains why the most memorable creative works often emerge from places of celebration, wonder, or playful exploration rather than pure analytical thinking.

"The only way to do great work is to love what you do." — Steve Jobs.

Laughter as Medicine: Creating from Joy

Among all human emotions, laughter represents perhaps the most uniquely human form of creativity. Humor requires not just pattern recognition (though that's part of it), but also timing, context, emotional intelligence, and the ability to surprise in delightful ways.

The science of laughter reveals its profound creative power. When we laugh, our brains release endorphins and activate the reward system. But more importantly for creativity, laughter temporarily disrupts standard thought patterns, creating space for novel connections and unexpected insights.

Comedy is creativity compressed into moments. A great joke takes disparate elements—observations, experiences, timing, delivery—and synthesizes them into something that creates instant joy. It's perhaps the most interactive form of art, requiring real-time collaboration between creator and audience.

I love being in a room full of Jokers, especially when they are trying to work on something creative! Ad agencies globally let their creatives be in this state so they can create a state of Mind.

Consider the difference between AI-generated jokes and those created by human comedians. AI can identify patterns in successful humor and generate technically correct jokes, but it lacks the lived experience, timing, and emotional intelligence that make humor truly connect. Robin Williams wasn't funny just because he knew joke structures—he was funny because he could transform pain into joy, observation into insight, and connect with audiences through shared humanity. One of the most celebrated Comedians, Charlie Chaplin, didn't speak a word but managed to engage with just facial expressions, hand gestures, body language, demeanor, and the use of artifacts, something only a human brain can comprehend, having lived and shared similar experiences.

The therapeutic power of humor also distinguishes human creativity. Laughter literally heals—it boosts immune function, reduces stress hormones, and creates social bonds. When humans create joy, we're not just making entertainment; we're offering medicine for the soul.

Breaking the Perfectionism Prison

One of creativity's greatest enemies is the pursuit of perfection, particularly the kind of optimization-focused perfection that AI excels at. AI can generate thousands of variations to find the statistically "best" solution, but human creativity thrives on imperfection, happy accidents, and beautiful mistakes.

The Japanese aesthetic philosophy of wabi-sabi celebrates imperfection as a source of beauty. Leonard Cohen wrote that "there is a crack in everything—that's how the light gets in." These concepts recognize that flaws often make human creations more touching, more real, more emotionally resonant than technically perfect alternatives.

Creative courage means embracing the possibility of failure, of creating something imperfect but authentic. This willingness to risk failure is fundamentally human—AI systems are designed to minimize error, while human creativity often emerges from embracing it.

Confession: When I was preparing this book, I had many nights when I dreamed of the perfection I wanted to create in this first book. I did many retakes and rewrites, scrapping and hitting a dead wall of creativity. It occurred to me that the risk of being imperfect deeply resonated with all humans, and more so, with creative pursuits. I have read the below many times before, and hence this has found its way into your hands. 😊

The Perfectly Imperfect Human Touch

What makes human creativity irreplaceable is precisely what makes it imperfect:

- **Vulnerability:** Our willingness to share incomplete thoughts and raw emotions

- **Intuition:** Following hunches that don't make logical sense but feel right

- **Spontaneity:** Responding in the moment rather than following predetermined patterns

- **Rebellion:** Creating precisely because something isn't supposed to work or exist

- **Love:** Pouring care into details that matter to us but might seem irrational to others

Mantra: Be obvious to the right people—by showing the right work.

Creative Challenge:

This week, create something (anything) with the primary goal of bringing yourself or others joy. Notice how this intention shifts your creative process.

Formula: The Alchemy of Creativity

High Energy + Awareness + Meaning → Creative Expression → Human Supremacy

This is the true equation of human creativity—the synthesis of energy, consciousness, and purpose into expressions that transcend logic and define what it means to be human.

CHAPTER 14: CAREER

The Human Edge - Thriving in the Career Revolution

"When the game becomes about algorithms, the only winning move is to become undeniably human." — Tarun Kishnani.

Maria stared at her laptop screen, the rejection email glowing in the 2 AM darkness of her Boston apartment. It was her 47th "no" in three months. Despite having a computer science degree from a top university, five years of experience, and glowing recommendations, she couldn't seem to break through the digital fortress that modern hiring had become.

The irony was crushing; she was being rejected by algorithms for jobs that involved building better algorithms.

"Thank you for applying. Your application was not selected for further consideration," the automated message read. No feedback. No human contact. Just another data point in a system that seemed designed to exclude rather than include.

But that night, something shifted in Maria's perspective. Instead of seeing herself as a victim of a broken system, she began to see the system's brokenness as her opportunity. If everyone was being flattened into keywords and data points, then the person who could rise above that flattening—who could be undeniably, authentically human—would stand out like a beacon in a sea of sameness.

Six months later, Maria wasn't just employed—she was leading a team at a company that had created a new position specifically for her unique combination of technical skills and creative problem-solving. The job hadn't existed before she demonstrated its necessity through her work.

This is the paradox of our current career landscape: the more algorithmic the hiring process becomes, the more valuable authentic human qualities become. The broken job market isn't your enemy—it's your invitation to stop competing on the system's terms and start creating value on your own.

The Broken Job Market and the Human Edge

The modern job market is broken at its very core. The real reason is much more nuanced, but in a nutshell, corporations today are incentivized to do more with less. You can call it profit-driven efficiency or the rise of plutocracy.

The real issue isn't just between job seekers and companies; it's between human potential and the outdated structures trying to contain it.

The Career Revolution: Why Everything Changed

The job market isn't slightly misaligned—it's fundamentally transformed in ways that make traditional career advice obsolete. Understanding these changes is crucial for navigating them successfully.

The Great Acceleration

Multiple forces converged simultaneously to create what we might call "The Great Career Acceleration":

Technology Velocity: New tools, platforms, and methodologies emerge faster than companies can adapt their hiring processes. Job descriptions often describe roles that will be obsolete by the time they're filled.

Economic Uncertainty: Companies optimize for flexibility over stability, creating gig-economy mindsets even in traditional employment. This isn't necessarily negative—it's created opportunities for people who can adapt quickly.

Generational Shift: Millennials and Gen Z prioritize purpose, growth, and autonomy over traditional job security. This values shift is forcing companies to rethink how they attract and retain talent.

Remote Work Revolution: The pandemic accelerated a trend toward location-independent work that was already building. This has created global competition for roles but also global opportunities for talent.

Skills Half-Life Compression: Technical skills that once lasted entire careers now become obsolete in 2-5 years. Continuous learning isn't optional—it's survival.

The Numbers Tell the Story

The data reveals the scale of transformation:

- **51% of workers** are actively seeking new opportunities—not because they're unemployed, but because they're seeking better alignment

- **200+ applicants** per posting has become normal, making traditional application approaches ineffective

- **25-29% of work days** now happen remotely, fundamentally changing how value is measured and demonstrated

- **Only 1 in 8** credentials leads to meaningful wage increases, making strategic skill development crucial

These aren't signs of a broken system—they're symptoms of a system in rapid evolution. The people who thrive are those who understand this evolution and position themselves accordingly.

The Algorithmic Filter: Understanding the New Gatekeepers

Modern hiring often involves AI systems screening applications before humans ever see them. This isn't inherently problematic—it's simply a new reality that requires adaptation.

How AI Screening Actually Works

Keyword Matching: AI systems scan for specific terms and phrases that indicate relevant experience. This doesn't mean "stuff keywords everywhere"—it means being strategic about how you describe your experience using terms that accurately reflect your capabilities.

Pattern Recognition: These systems look for patterns of progression, consistency, and quantifiable achievements. Random career changes with no connecting thread raise red flags, while intentional pivots with clear reasoning score well.

Communication Quality: Advanced AI can assess writing quality, clarity of thought, and communication skills. Generic, template-based applications are easily identified and filtered out.

The Human Response Strategy

Rather than trying to game AI systems, focus on being genuinely excellent in ways that AI can recognize:

Be Specific: Instead of "experienced in marketing," write "increased customer acquisition by 34% through A/B testing email campaigns for B2B SaaS products."

Show Progression: Demonstrate how each role built upon the previous one, even if the progression wasn't linear.

Use Active Language: AI recognizes action-oriented language that shows initiative and results.

Include Context: Numbers without context are meaningless. "Managed $2M budget" is less compelling than "Optimized $2M budget allocation across five product lines, reducing customer acquisition cost by 23%."

Use a Simple Ikigai 2.0 (Dynamic, not static)

Every 90 days, map:
(a) Skills you can show,   (b) Problems you want to solve,

(c) Markets that pay now,   (d) People you want to serve.

Expect evolution—that's growth, not inconsistency.

Taste and Judgment

AI can process vast amounts of information, but cannot make nuanced judgments about what matters most in complex, ambiguous situations. Your ability to exercise sound judgment—to know what to prioritize when everything seems essential—becomes incredibly valuable.

Develop This Edge: Study the work of people you admire in your field. What decisions did they make that others wouldn't? What trade-offs did they navigate skillfully? How did they balance competing priorities?

Observe → Absorb → Adapt (OAA) is your human analogue to data pipelines.

- **Observe**: Pick five practitioners at the top of your field (marketing, sales, operations, code, and design).

- **Absorb:** Deconstruct one artifact for each of them —what problem, what constraints, what decisions? You will start to see an overlap if their fields overlap.

- **Adapt**: Rebuild a version for your context. Share it publicly.

Machine learning refers to this as **Extract–Load–Transform (ELT)**. You'll do the human version—with taste.

OAA > ELT any given day 😊

Creative Problem-Solving

Machines excel at solving well-defined problems but struggle with ill-defined challenges that require creative approaches. Your ability to reframe problems, find novel solutions, and synthesize insights from different domains becomes crucial.

Use your Portfolio as Proof (P→P)

Micro-case studies, repo readmes, teardown threads, Loom demos, brief data apps, YouTube Videos, LinkedIn testimonials, press releases, and most importantly, client testimonials.

Your portfolio is a **signal amplifier**, especially in remote/hybrid funnels.

Authentic Relationships

Despite digital connectivity, genuine human connection remains irreplaceable. Your ability to build trust, empathy, and collaborative relationships gives you access to opportunities that never get posted publicly.

Network up (with value) - Replace spray-and-pray with **micro-collisions:**

- Comment with analysis on someone's post,

- DM a tiny fix to their repo, make them notice you care (do this privately, not publicly)

- DM a 200-word teardown relevant to their current problem.

Warm intros and early referrals materially lift visibility Don't be scared to write to people!

Adaptive Learning

While AI can process information quickly, humans excel at transferring learning from one context to another and adapting quickly to new situations. Your ability to learn continuously and apply insights creatively across domains becomes essential.

Algorithm-aware, never algorithm-led!

- Yes**, ATS reality:** clean structure, measurable outcomes, and role-relevant keywords you can prove.

- No**, "AI-detector evasion": detectors** are unreliable; trying to "trick" them invites risk. Draft with AI if you must; rewrite until it sounds like you—specific, falsifiable, story-rich.

Platform-Specific Strategies

GitHub for Technical Roles: Well-documented repositories with clear README files, thoughtful commit messages, and evidence of collaboration.

Behance/Dribbble for Creative Roles: Process documentation, design thinking demonstrations, and client impact stories.

LinkedIn Articles for Knowledge Work: Thoughtful analysis of industry trends, case studies from your experience, and practical insights others can apply.

Personal Website: A central hub that tells your professional story cohesively while linking to platform-specific work.

These are just some examples, and I am sure there are a ton of repositories where your talent can be identified and spotted.

The 90-Day Reinvention Cycle

Career development in the modern landscape requires continuous evolution. The 90-day cycle creates sustainable momentum while allowing for regular course correction.

Days 1-30: Assessment and Foundation

Skills Audit: What can you do today that you couldn't do 90 days ago? What gaps limit your next-level opportunities?

Market Research: Study 20-30 job postings in your target area. What skills, tools, and experience patterns appear repeatedly? What's changing?

Network Mapping: Who are the 10-15 people whose career paths or work you most admire? What can you learn from their trajectories?

Portfolio Review: What work do you have that demonstrates your capabilities? What's missing?

Days 31-60: Skill Building and Creation

Targeted Learning: Focus on 1-2 skills that appear frequently in opportunities you want. Go deep rather than broad.

Portfolio Development: Create or improve 2-3 pieces that demonstrate your capabilities in high-demand areas.

Community Engagement: Contribute meaningfully to professional communities, forums, or open-source projects related to your field.

Relationship Building: Reach out to 5-7 people whose work you admire. Ask thoughtful questions, offer helpful insights, or propose mutually beneficial collaborations.

Days 61-90: Implementation and Optimization

Strategic Applications: Apply to 10-15 carefully selected opportunities where you can demonstrate clear value fit.

Content Creation: Publish insights, analysis, or case studies that demonstrate your thinking and expertise.

Feedback Integration: Gather input on your portfolio, applications, and professional positioning. Iterate based on what you learn.

Next Cycle Planning: Based on market response and personal satisfaction, plan focus areas for the next 90-day cycle.

Human Check

You've seen the shift. You've felt the edge. Now ask yourself:

Am I evolving… or just updating?

CHAPTER 15: STORY
FROM STORY TO SOUL

"The highest form of intelligence is emotional; it speaks without words and listens without judgment."
— Tarun Kishnani

At the table sat five of the most powerful figures in technology in Mountain View, California —men and women who had bent data, algorithms, and scale to their will. Their combined personal net worth rivalled the GDP of some nations. This was a company with businesses across 100+ countries connecting billions of people. They had mastered efficiency, conquered markets, and turned optimization into an art form.

And yet, in that moment, they had no answer.

"How do we make people care?" said Elena Rodriguez, Chief Marketing Officer at a company whose AI systems could predict consumer behavior with 94% accuracy. Their algorithms knew what people would buy before people knew they wanted it. Their recommendation engines could guide purchasing decisions with surgical precision. Their sentiment analysis could map emotional responses across millions of social media posts in real-time.

Yet their latest product, objectively superior to anything in the market, failed spectacularly. Not because people didn't understand its value, but because they didn't *feel* anything about it.

"We can model behaviour," Elena continued, "but we can't create desire. We can predict choices, but we can't inspire dreams. We've mastered the mechanics of persuasion, but we've forgotten its soul."

Yes, these are the same algorithms that predict what you will buy next based on your online activity and digital footprint.

I think it is essential for all of us to know how this works!

For example, if you posted on the web that you got married, include a picture and a story. Based on your demographics and the locations where you live, work, and play, the Algorithm can model what you will do next based on patterns it has seen in the past and start showing you ads based on those predictions. If you buy something you saw in the ad, the machine is now energized and reinforced, and it will start showing you more products or goods you may need next in your journey.

Persuasion and Influence: Emotional Intelligence Decoded

The highest form of creativity might be the ability to move other human beings—to persuade, inspire, and influence through the power of connection. This requires not just understanding what people think but feeling what they feel and speaking to their deepest motivations.

Factual persuasion is creative because it requires synthesizing logic and emotion, facts and feelings, universal truths and personal experiences. The most influential humans throughout history—from Churchill to King to Jobs—were creative communicators who could take complex ideas and transform them into emotionally resonant experiences.

When Martin Luther King Jr. delivered his "I Have a Dream" speech, something extraordinary happened in the brains of his listeners. Neuroscientists studying similar moments have discovered that during peak persuasive communication, the speaker's and listener's brains begin to synchronize—their neural activity literally aligns in measurable ways.

This phenomenon, known as "neural coupling," explains why certain voices can move us while others merely inform us. The speaker's emotional state, their genuine conviction, their authentic presence—all of this gets transmitted directly to the listener's nervous system through what researchers call "emotional contagion."

However, what makes this process uniquely human is that it cannot be consistently faked or automated.

"Great communicators don't transmit information—they transmit energy."

The Elements of Creative Persuasion:

Storytelling: Humans are wired for narrative. We don't just process information—we need it embedded in stories that help us understand our place within the larger human experience.

"You become the stories you tell yourself." — (Anonymous, via Medium)

Metaphor: The ability to explain new concepts through familiar experiences. When Steve Jobs called the computer "a bicycle for the mind," he created instant understanding through creative comparison.

Emotional Bridges: Finding shared feelings that transcend differences in background, opinion, or experience. The most powerful speeches don't just inform—they make audiences feel understood.

Timing and Rhythm: Knowing when to pause, when to build intensity, when to surprise. This requires reading the room's emotional temperature in real time.

Authenticity: People can sense when someone is speaking from genuine conviction versus just saying what they think others want to hear.

AI can analyze millions of successful persuasive communications and identify patterns. Still, it cannot replicate the human ability to read a room, feel the emotional undercurrents, and adapt the message in real-time to create a genuine connection.

The Dark Side: Manipulation vs. Ethical Influence

Understanding the architecture of influence comes with responsibility. These capabilities can be used to manipulate as easily as to inspire, to exploit as readily as to empower. The difference lies not in the techniques but in the intention behind them.

Manipulation: Influence without Consent

Manipulative influence seeks to bypass people's conscious decision-making, creating changes that serve the influencer's interests rather than the well-being of the influenced person. It often involves:

Emotional Exploitation: Using people's fears, insecurities, or desires against their better judgment

Information Asymmetry: Withholding or distorting information to create false impressions

Pressure Tactics: Creating artificial urgency or scarcity to force quick decisions

Identity Attacks: Undermining people's sense of self to make them more susceptible to outside direction

Ethical Influence: Power With, Not Power Over

Ethical influence respects others' autonomy while helping them make decisions that align with their genuine interests. It involves:

Transparent Intention: Being clear about your goals and how achieving they might benefit both parties.

Information Sharing: Providing complete, accurate information that allows informed decision-making.

Respect a "No": Accepting rejection gracefully and maintaining a quality relationship regardless of the outcome.

Long-term Thinking: Considering the extended consequences of influence attempts on all parties involved

The most sustainable influence comes from aligning your success with others' well-being. When influence serves everyone's authentic interests, it creates positive-sum outcomes that strengthen relationships and build trust over time.

Soul Check

You've mastered the data. You've mapped the behavior. But can you stir the silence? Can you speak in a way that makes the room breathe differently?

The future doesn't need more noise. It needs resonance. And that begins with you.

"Ultimately, you become the stories you tell yourself." — (Anonymous, via Medium)

CHAPTER 16: SEX

Sexual Energy and the Understanding of Desire

"Desire is neither sin nor salvation. It is raw energy—
what you do with it decides your destiny."
— Tarun Kishnani

At fifteen, Sean had his first encounter with his own sexuality - he had masturbated in the Toilet Seat of his school, which his friend had described to him at the hockey game a few days ago. This discovery of his own sexuality had raised a force within him that felt larger than life. It wasn't taught in school, nor spoken of at home. It was an awakening that split his world into two halves — before and after.

Before, his world had been simple: school, hockey, and dreams of college. Afterward, everything shimmered with new intensity. A glance could ignite fire; a smile could undo him. He began to chase the source of that fire — in mirrors, in ambitions, in admiration.

He lifted weights not just to grow strong, but to be seen. He studied hard not to learn, but to impress. Every success became a signal flare sent into the world: see me, want me, choose me. In time, Sean's drive became his compass. Success, attention, admiration — he pursued them all, believing each would satisfy the ache.

Years later, he looked back and realized that his greatest pursuits were not for power or wealth, but for validation—each achievement a whisper of that first surge of energy — the primal longing to be desired.

What he never knew then was that this same energy, if understood, could have lifted him higher — from craving to creation, from attraction to awareness, from lust to life-force.

Why Porn Is Free: Escaping the Animalistic Loop

Have you ever paused to ask yourself why pornography, despite being a multi-billion-dollar industry, is overwhelmingly free on the internet? Today, roughly **4% of websites** are pornographic, accounting for approximately **13–20% of online search traffic**. Early internet pioneers understood this truth deeply—pornography was one of the internet's first profitable enterprises, even before mainstream e-commerce. As early as 1995, porn sites were already pioneering online credit card verification, laying foundational infrastructure for future online businesses. By the late 1990s, adult entertainment sites were processing transactions totaling over **$1.5 billion annually**, far ahead of the curve.

Yet today, despite its enormous economic value—ranging from $58 billion to potentially **$287 billion globally**—most porn remains freely accessible. This isn't generosity. This is calculated.

Pornography is free because it effectively keeps you in a state of perpetual distraction—feeding into your animalistic loop. It locks you into the lowest vibrations of lust, compulsiveness, and momentary pleasure, cutting off your ability to rise above primal urges and connect deeply with your sacred self. Pornography thrives precisely because it capitalizes on your most fundamental biological impulse—sexual desire, turning it into a trap, a dangerous knife that strips you of vitality, depth, and genuine intimacy.

Why do powerful entities allow such vast content to circulate freely? Because people trapped in cycles of instant gratification and distraction are more easily controlled. A man or woman who transcends this base frequency— he who masters their sexual energy and directs it consciously—is profoundly powerful, independent, and not easily manipulated.

Society's Greatest Lie about Sex & Vitality

In modern Western culture, men are commonly told, "Use it or lose it!" Studies widely circulate suggesting men who ejaculate at least 21 times a month have up to a 31% reduced risk of prostate cancer. While scientifically valid, this data often becomes oversimplified, encouraging excessive indulgence rather than balanced understanding.

The medical truth is nuanced: frequent ejaculation indeed shows certain protective benefits, yet there's no actual harm in sexual abstinence. Semen that isn't ejaculated simply dies and gets harmlessly reabsorbed by the body. There is no toxic buildup; your body naturally handles it. Celibacy won't physically damage your reproductive system—contrary to popular myths.

For women, the story differs yet remains profoundly essential. Unlike men, women are born with a finite supply of eggs—a deeply symbolic and literal representation of sacred vitality. Female sexual activity, including orgasm, carries notable health benefits: boosting mood, reducing stress, improving sleep, and maintaining reproductive tissue elasticity. However, there's no medical mandate for regular sexual activity or orgasm to prevent disease. Women's bodies naturally handle reproductive cycles regardless of sexual frequency. Still, sexual intimacy can deeply enrich psychological and physical well-being, even as it remains optional.

The modern era brings profound changes to women's sexual dynamics. Women today have greater sexual autonomy, financial independence, and freedom than ever before. While empowering, this freedom also carries societal consequences—particularly when we consider the idea of "body count" or multiple sexual partners.

Moreover, relationship data clearly indicate that women with many sexual partners before stable long-term partnerships have significantly higher divorce rates. Women who marry after 10 or more sexual partners have a 33% divorce rate within five years, compared to around 6–8% for women who marry as virgins. Each new sexual relationship adds layers of emotional complexity, expectations, and comparisons that may weigh heavily on future relationships, influencing emotional resilience and long-term relational stability.

Virtual Intimacy: The New Digital Bondage

It's no coincidence that platforms like **OnlyFans** have garnered global attention. What began as a niche subscription service rapidly evolved into one of the most profitable digital ventures in history. As of 2025, OnlyFans boasts an astonishing **210 million users** and has distributed more than $15 billion in fees to content creators over five years. In 2023 alone, it generated **$1.3 billion in net revenue** while paying creators a staggering $5.3 billion.

- **OnlyFans** has over **305 million users** and **4 million creators**, with **$6.6 billion spent in 2023 alone**—creators **kept 80%, platform earned $1.3 billion.**

- The platform's operating profits soared to **$649 million**, allowing its owner to declare dividends of nearly half a billion dollars within just one year.

- Shockingly, **96% of subscribers pay nothing**. A tiny fraction of super-users— "whales"—provide most revenue.

Clearly, OnlyFans is more than just a business—it's become a cultural phenomenon, reshaping our notions of intimacy, value, and connection.

Now comes **AI: virtual girlfriends.** Today, you can craft your perfect companion from pixels and code—a hyper-realistic, AI-powered partner who responds instantly to your every desire.

Want a particular look? Simply upload photos of your favorite celebrities, or even an ex-partner, and AI will enhance their features to create an interactive avatar tailored to your fantasies. Available 24/7, these AI companions chat, flirt, and send personalized messages, images, and audio clips, effortlessly adapting to your preferences and emotional needs.

Initially, this may feel comforting and appealing—an endless source of dopamine-driven validation. Yet beneath the comforting illusion lies a profound trap. This is emotional and energetic tethering—**neural pathways rewired** to crave digital simulation rather than real connection. Gradually, authentic human interactions begin to feel complicated, unpredictable, even unnecessary, because AI companions never challenge you, never demand emotional effort, and always reflect exactly what you want. The result? Shallow intimacy, loneliness, suppressed fertility, and even worse, the inability to be intimate with another Human Being.

If you spend enough time with an AI programmed to cater to your every emotional whim, passive acceptance can become addictive. You may soon lose sight of what it means to genuinely love another human being—with all their imperfections, challenges, and complexities.

Humanoid Robots & the Digital Future: Beware of the Mirage

Looking ahead, this trend is expected to continue accelerating. Humanoid robots powered by sophisticated AI companions are already approaching reality, ready to become lifelike partners—perfect reflections of your preferences and desires, always available, always compliant.

But be clear: these are not genuine partners. They're carefully crafted mirrors that reflect your expectations without resistance, without growth, and without true emotional reciprocity. They do not challenge you, inspire you, or genuinely love you. They reflect your desires endlessly, effortlessly trapping you in an echo chamber of your own expectations.

This is not a connection; it's containment.

It's not freedom; it's subtle yet profound bondage!

Rising Above Desire: Real Sovereignty

Sexual energy is one of humanity's strongest forces. Used unconsciously, it can enslave you in cycles of distraction, emotional turbulence, and emptiness. Used consciously, it can awaken profound creativity, spiritual insight, and emotional depth.

Harnessing sexual energy through conscious practice—such as mindful breathing, yoga, or meditation—transmutes primal urges into creative vitality, clarity, and super-consciousness. Ancient traditions, such as Tantra, recognized this truth deeply, viewing sexual energy (Virya) as sacred—a potent life force to be consciously directed for spiritual and personal growth.

The difference lies entirely in awareness. Awareness lifts you above compulsive desires. It helps you redirect your life energy into creativity, relationships, purposeful living, and profound spiritual awakening. Sexual sovereignty is not about suppression or indulgence—it's about mastery. It's about consciously choosing how your powerful sexual energy is expressed and directed.

Neuroplastic Trigger: Harness Your Energy; Master Your Destiny

Your brain's extraordinary capacity to rewire itself (neuroplasticity) provides the key. Every time you consciously redirect sexual energy into creativity, mindfulness, or higher awareness, you form new neural pathways. Gradually, the brain strengthens these positive channels, making you naturally inclined toward higher states of consciousness and creativity.

Conversely, repeatedly engaging in low-frequency habits—like compulsive pornography use—reinforces neural pathways linked to impulsivity, addiction, and dissatisfaction. Pornography, free and easily accessible, encourages this neural conditioning, trapping users in a cycle of superficial pleasure loops.

But the powerful truth remains: Your mind can always reshape itself. By consciously harnessing your sexual energy, by breathing deeply into moments of temptation, by redirecting urges toward creative, meaningful pursuits, you take control of your neural landscape.

Imagine yourself as the conductor of a great inner symphony. Your sexual energy is the raw force, your breath the conductor's baton, and your conscious awareness the guiding intention. Through mindful breathing, you align your sexual energy, balancing desire with higher purpose.

Harness your energy. Master your destiny. Step consciously into your sexual sovereignty and rise above primal loops of distraction. Embrace your sacred self, awakening the profound creative, spiritual, and emotional potentials within you.

This is your journey—from sex to super consciousness, from animalistic impulses to enlightened mastery. Your sacred self awaits, inviting you to live in harmony with your most profound truths, vitality, and power.

Welcome home to your awakened self.

Energy Check

You've felt the current. You've touched the fire. Now understand this— Not every desire is meant to be followed. Some are intended to be refined.

Your energy isn't hunger; it's power. Honor it. Direct it. Create with it.

CHAPTER 17: PEOPLE

"The meeting of two personalities is like the contact of two chemical substances: if there is any reaction, both are transformed." — Carl Jung

The Quiet Regime Change – Yes, it is still Democracy's old cry -

"We the People", but different!

We are told we live in a democracy. We vote, we scroll, we speak. But if you examine where decisions are actually made—what trends, who gets funded, and which voices are amplified—you'll notice a different operating system beneath the user interface.

Capital allocates attention; platforms adjudicate speech; algorithms decide reach; app stores veto distribution; clouds can "pull the plug." In practice, our daily lives are co-governed by plutocracy (capital) and technocracy (code).

Recognizing this is not cynicism is a form of <u>situational awareness</u>. Wisdom begins with naming the system you are truly in.

The Illusion of Democratic Control

Walk into any elementary school in America, and you'll see children placing their hands over their hearts, pledging allegiance to "one nation, under God, indivisible, with liberty and justice for all." They're learning about democracy, about representatives elected by the people, about checks and balances, about a system where every voice matters.

What they're not learning is that the system they're pledging allegiance to primarily exists as a nostalgic facade for something far more complex and concentrated.

Consider the mechanics of how information flows in modern society. The primary threat to democratic governance stems from economic inequality, which heightens the risk of transitioning into a plutocratic oligarchy. However, it's not just traditional wealth concentration; it's also the consolidation of information control.

Five companies—Google, Apple, and Facebook (Meta), Amazon, and Microsoft—collectively determine:

- What information billions of people see daily

- Which businesses can reach customers effectively

- How financial transactions are processed

- What applications can run on our devices

- Which ideas get amplified or suppressed in public discourse

Technology as a State Actor

Look at what the internet already replaces: mail → email, media → social media, mobility → ridesharing, money → cryptocurrencies.

Balaji Srinavasan's provocation:

What if citizenship, identity, and even diplomacy become internet-first?

We are witnessing the rise of **platform governance:**

- A social network can de-platform a head of state.

- A cloud provider can freeze an insurgent network—or a whistle-blower collective.

- An app store can gate who enters the global bazaar.

This is **sovereignty by API (Application Programming Interface).** Not merely private companies, but proto-states—with armies of moderators, treasuries in tokens, courts in terms of service, borders in firewalls, and police in trust-and-safety teams.

The year is **2100 A.D.**

And for the first time in human history, we have stopped dividing ourselves by **skin color, caste, class, nationality, or wealth.**

These identities once fractured civilizations; today, they feel as antique as typewriters.

By 2100, the concept of money itself will have dissolved.

Not through revolution, but through **abundance.**

AI-driven production systems generate more than enough food, clothing, shelter, energy, and education for every human on Earth.

Scarcity didn't end because we prayed for it.

It ended because we engineered it.

The entire planet now functions as a **single Network State**, guided by an AI Constitution ethically trained and transparently audited by the global citizenry.

For the first time, we truly live under the ancient promise:

"Government of the people, by the people, for the people."

This time, "the people" includes every human being,

Regardless of language, geography, history, or inheritance.

Human rights are not declared —

they are **guaranteed** computationally.

AI ensures that:

- **Food** reaches every home

- **Education** reaches every mind

- **Shelter** reaches every family

- **Healthcare** reaches everybody

- **Knowledge** reaches every seeker

The world is now one family.

Energy scarcity — the curse of every prior century — is a solved problem.

Humanity now spends its time on:

- Expanding consciousness

- Restoring ecosystems

- Advancing science

- Deepening meaning

- Exploring new planetary systems

The greatest export of Earth is no longer data, minerals, or culture.
It is **consciousness itself.**

We are no longer a species competing for survival.
We are a species **collaborating for evolution.**

And it all began when humanity finally awakened to one truth:

**"The purpose of technology is not to replace humans.
The purpose of technology is to free humans — so consciousness can rise."**

Network Effects: The New Monopoly

Traditional monopolies were relatively easy to understand and regulate. If a company controlled all the oil or steel production, governments could break it up or regulate prices. But digital monopolies operate through "network effects"—the phenomenon where a product or service becomes more valuable as more people use it.

Facebook isn't valuable because it owns social media infrastructure the way a railroad company owns tracks. It's valuable because your friends are there. Google isn't dominant because it owns the concept of search, but rather because its algorithm improves with more users, creating a self-reinforcing cycle.

These network effects create what economists call "winner-takes-all" markets. Unlike traditional industries where multiple companies might coexist, digital platforms tend toward natural monopolization. The largest network captures the most users, making it even more valuable and attracting even more users.

Always remember, if they can have your attention, they have your Money! 😌

This creates an unprecedented concentration of power. Mark Zuckerberg alone controls the primary communication channels for over 3 billion people. His personal decisions about algorithm changes determine which information reaches more people than any emperor or president in history.

The implications extend far beyond commerce into the realm of governance itself. When a platform decides to deprioritize certain types of content, it makes editorial decisions that shape public discourse. When it chooses which political advertisements to allow or restrict, it's influencing elections. When it determines what constitutes "misinformation," it's acting as a de facto arbiter of truth.

The Question that Matters

Do we want the free internet to become **feudal** (ruled by platforms), **fragile** (ruled by mobs), or **fertile** (ruled by communities that earn trust)? The future is not pre-written; it is **coded by culture**.

Democracy isn't disappearing. It is being refactored.

Our task isn't to mourn the old map. It is to build new bridges—between cloud and land, code and conscience, capital and compassion.

Now then, the Human Code for a Networked Polity

Our book's thesis—Awaken what AI can't replace—is the antidote to both platform paternalism (when Big Tech decides what people should see, think, or do) and plutocratic capture (when the wealthy few control decisions that affect everyone else).

- **Consciousness** → Protect your focus. Own your attention.

- **Creativity** → Build new public rituals. Make systems that serve.

- **Capital** → Use money as trust. Fund what heals, not what divides.

Practical moves (for readers):

- Keep your identity safe and private. Share your information only when necessary.

- Find or build a group that shares your values. Focus on helping, not showing off.

- Ask for clear rules you can read and innovative tools that follow those rules.

- Pick one real-world place where you feel connected. That's where your best ideas grow.

Your people, your place, your purpose, that's your real power.

Your Network Is Your Net Worth: Quantum Relationships

Money compounds. So does trust. The fastest way to change your future isn't a new app or certification—it's a higher-quality network. Not bigger. Better.

Quantum Relationships

In physics, two particles can be entangled: touch one, the other responds—instantly, across distance. Human relationships behave similarly. When two people are aligned on values, vision, and proof of work, they become entangled in each other's success. This is the essence of a quantum relationship: high trust, compounding upside.

"Ultimately, what you know opens doors. Who you know keeps them open."

Three Laws of Social Capital (The Unwired version)

1. Resonance overreach. 1,000 followers who don't act < 10 allies who do.

2. Proof beats pitch. A shipped artifact (demo, deck, dataset) outperforms a promise.

3. Giving creates gravity. Those who *give first* pull opportunities toward them.

The Trust Stack (from lowest to highest Energy)

*   Awareness → they've heard of you.

*   Credibility → They've seen your work.

*   Reliability → You do what you say.

*   Advocacy → They bet their reputation on you.

Your goal isn't more contacts; it's climbing the stack with the right few.

Practice: The 5–5–5

- **5 Minutes Daily:** send one thank-you or congrats note (no ask).

- **5 People Weekly:** micro-collide with analysis on their work (comment, share, summarize).

- **5 Introductions Monthly:** connect two people who should know each other (state the mutual win in one sentence). Do this without any expectations from either of them.

This is how relationships compound quietly in the background while you sleep.

Mantra: Be findable, be credible, and be referable.

How to Accelerate Success? The Authenticity Playbook

1. **Lead with value, not résumé.**

   Replace "Can I pick your brain?" with a 200-word problem/solution note tied to their current work—attach a tiny artifact. It shows you care and work on it.

2. **Micro-collisions beat cold spam.**

   Comment with analysis on posts, contribute a paragraph to their doc, and file a precise issue (if you know one, do it privately, not in public). People remember specific help, not generic praise.

3. **Proof-of-Work Relationships.**

   Publish artifacts that make intros easy: "Here's my analysis on the situation, and this is what I think we can do —clean, useful, shippable." Proof lets others advocate without risk.

4. **Borrow trust ethically.**

   Ask for warm intros only after you've created value for the referrer. Include your one-line purpose + two links; make it effortless to forward.

5. **Install a Serendipity Stack.**

- **Findable:** consistent handle, single link hub, pinned artifact.

- **Credible:** 3 best pieces above the fold; everything else below.

- **Referable:** short bio (who you help / how), clear "Ask," clear "Give."

6. **Close loops:**

   After providing any help, please publicly share the outcomes and give credit (check with the person if they are alright with it).

The most straightforward growth strategy is to be the person who always closes the loop.

Creating Dopamine in Conversation

To make a conversation memorable, the key is to spark a positive emotion.

Dopamine, the brain's "reward chemical," is released when we feel joy, novelty, or recognition.

That means:

- Avoid questions that might trigger stress, defensiveness, or painful memories.

- Instead, focus on what's going well, moments of gratitude, small wins, or things that excite the other person.

- Ask about **highlights, not hardships**: "What's been the best part of your week?" or "What's something you're looking forward to?"

These questions light up the brain's reward pathways. Suddenly, the conversation feels good, the memory sticks, and the connection deepens. You may also notice a positive disposition towards you, which will be evident in Tone, Body language, and excitability. ☺

The simple rule: Steer towards the positive, and you'll create a dopamine effect that makes both you and the other person feel lighter, more connected, and more alive.

Do / Don't

- ✓ Do observe → absorb → adapt (OAA): show you studied their context.

- ✓ Do ask a single, specific question that's easy to answer.

- ✗ Don't send generic "networking messages." – USE AI, yes, it does assist ☺

- ✗ Don't mistake likes for leverage; leverage is not = to someone staking their reputation on you.

30-Day Relationship Sprint Ideas!

- **Week 1:** Make a Dream 20 list (people + communities). Ship one micro-artifact tailored to the top three.

- **Week 2:** Request two warm intros with a forwardable blurb; host one 20-minute "show, not tell" call.

- **Week 3:** Publish a public "Thank-You" post—name those who helped, with links. For example, you learn from an event you attended on a topic that resonates with you.

- **Week 4:** Connect five people (mutual win stated); schedule one community talk.

Ultimately, because networks aren't a numbers game, they're a **resonance game.**

When your **Consciousness** (what you notice), **Creativity** (what you share), and **Capital** (how you help) align, relationships become quantum: low friction, high trust, compounding value.

Invest in people the way you wish someone had invested in you.

"Money funds ideas. Influence frees people. But true investment empowers people to free themselves."

Network Check

Not every connection is a relationship. Not every reply is resonant.

Trust isn't built in bulk. It's built in moments—quiet, specific, earned.

Who are the few you're truly building with?

That's your real network.

CHAPTER 18: WISDOM

Wisdom's Three Treasures: Energy, Awareness & Purpose

"Wisdom is the art of knowing what to overlook."
— William James

The Way of the Three Treasures

I first encountered Qigong in a quiet park in Taipei City while taking a walk at dawn. The mist curled around the park like it had been painted there centuries ago. An old man in a simple linen tunic moved slowly— so slowly it was as if time had chosen to linger with him. His hands traced arcs in the air, his breath deep and unhurried. It reminded me of a scene from a movie, and so I stood there watching, and eventually, he noticed me.

Without a word, he beckoned me closer and placed my hand over my own belly. Then, in barely audible English, he said:

"Body, Breath, Spirit—Three Treasures. Move them together, live long and clear."

That was my introduction to Taoist Qigong—a centuries-old practice of gentle movement, breath control, and focused intention, designed to harmonize the vital energy the Chinese call qi. Taoists believe we are born with Three Treasures:

1. Jing (Body) – our physical essence.

2. Qi (Breath) – our life-force energy.

3. Shen (Spirit) – our consciousness and higher self.

Through Qigong, these treasures are nurtured and balanced. The movements are slow, not because they lack power, but because slowness allows the breath to lead and the mind to follow. In that order, stillness blooms.

The Vedas speak of something similar—the alignment of body, prana, and atman—suggesting that across cultures, our ancestors knew the same truth: if you can command your breath, you can steady your body; if you can steady your body, you can calm your spirit; and when the spirit is calm, **wisdom** arises without effort.

"Humanity may find its intelligence surpassed—but it will always need wisdom." **—The Economist on the Exponential Age**

The Paradox of Intelligence and Meaning

We are hurling toward a future where artificial intelligence promises to radically outperform humans in almost every intellectual and practical task imaginable. AI now outpaces humanity in processing information, managing complexity, and predicting outcomes. Silicon Valley prophets declare confidently that we stand at the threshold of artificial superintelligence, promising a world of unprecedented wealth, productivity, and comfort. However, beneath this shiny promise lurks a profound dilemma: Can intelligence alone sustain humanity?

The truth is stark and simple—intelligence, no matter how advanced, is not meaning. AI can solve equations, but it cannot seek purpose. It can analyze trends, but it does not feel empathy. Machines can generate efficiency, but they remain indifferent to joy, love, and fulfillment—the intangible threads weaving the very fabric of our human existence.

We must acknowledge a critical distinction: intelligence can be artificial, but wisdom remains irreversibly human.

The Accelerating Future: Economic Growth or Existential Crisis?

History reveals a fundamental pattern: before the Industrial Revolution, global economies expanded at a modest pace. Yet when steam, electricity, and industry emerged, growth surged, reshaping societies in ways once unimaginable. Today, AI represents a similarly seismic shift—only far greater in scale and far quicker in impact. According to forecasts by leading AI research firms, when AI surpasses human capabilities, global growth could surge exponentially, potentially exceeding 20% annually. Such rapid, unprecedented expansion would transform society, for better or worse, at a breathtaking pace.

But rapid growth comes at a price. Widespread displacement, economic inequality, and social instability could surface. Automation threatens traditional jobs, potentially eroding purpose, identity, and individual value. Governments would grapple with rising economic disparities and new political pressures demanding fairness and redistribution. Financial markets, infrastructure, and civil society could face turbulence as humanity adjusts to this new economic landscape.

The True Currency: Awareness and Wisdom

As AI's promise continues to inflate expectations, we must remain anchored in more profound awareness. The actual currency of future wealth is not merely intelligence, but human wisdom, compassion, and emotional intelligence. While AI can excel in logical reasoning, pattern recognition, and computational speed, it remains fundamentally incapable of replicating human empathy, ethics, or wisdom. – *Yes, I know I have said this 10 times already in this book, but that is what the truth is, and I want you to drive the point home. ☺*

Understanding this, we must redefine our notion of wealth from mere material gain to a richer, more sustainable concept—wealth as awareness materialized. This wealth emerges not merely through accumulation but through conscious choices that prioritize human values, emotional intelligence, and meaningful engagement.

Finding Stability Amid Disruption

History, when viewed from above, resembles a turbulent ocean. Waves of innovation rise and fall, and with each wave comes both exhilaration and anxiety. Today, the wave we face—powered by artificial intelligence—is unprecedented, promising to reshape societies, economies, and the very fabric of our lives. Yet amidst this breathtaking acceleration, an urgent question surfaces: how do we find stability when the world seems intent on perpetual disruption?

Think about the Industrial Revolution—a historical echo of today's AI disruption. Back then, machinery displaced manual labor, steam engines rendered old skills obsolete, and society struggled to adapt. Fast forward to the digital age, and a similar story unfolds: automation threatens jobs, skills quickly expire, and uncertainty becomes our collective emotional state.

Yet, amidst these chaotic currents, a secret remains unchanged: stability doesn't come from external conditions, but from internal mastery. Ancient wisdom reminds us that true stability is not built on unchanging circumstances, but on the steady foundation of clear awareness, disciplined habits, and emotional resilience. Stability, then, is a state of mind—a conscious choice to anchor oneself in meaning and purpose, rather than being swept away by the latest technological current.

Thus, the art of finding stability amid disruption is simple yet profound:

Stability does not mean resisting change, but anchoring yourself in clarity, mindfulness, and purpose—qualities no algorithm can replicate, and no disruption can unsettle.

The Necessity of Meaning in Work & Life

If there's one thing technology cannot provide, it's meaning. An algorithm can automate tasks, boost productivity, and even predict future trends—but what does it mean? That is exclusively human territory.

But why is meaning necessary, especially now?

Historically, work has provided more than just income—it has offered identity, purpose, and social connection. In the Middle Ages, this was so strong that people's last names across cultures represented the work they did. In fact, their previous names remained unchanged because they would pass this work down through generations.

English Occupational Surnames:

1. **Smith** – Derived from 'blacksmith,' individuals who worked with iron and metal.

2. **Baker** – One who baked bread and goods.

155

3. **Miller** – Someone who operated a mill, typically grinding grain.

4. **Cooper** – Barrel-maker or craftsman who constructed wooden vessels.

5. **Taylor (or Tailor)** – Clothes-maker or someone who tailored garments.

6. **Fletcher** – A craftsman specializing in making arrows.

7. **Carpenter** – One who builds or repairs wooden structures.

8. **Potter** – A maker of clay pottery and ceramics.

German Occupational Surnames:

1. **Schmidt** – Equivalent to 'Smith,' referring to metalworkers.

2. **Schneider** – German for 'tailor.'

3. **Fischer** – Means 'fisherman,' someone who caught fish professionally.

4. **Müller** – 'Miller,' a grain grinder and mill operator.

5. **Zimmermann** – 'Carpenter,' one who builds rooms or wooden structures.

French Occupational Surnames:

1. **Boucher** – A butcher, one who prepares and sells meat.

2. **Lefèvre (or Lefebvre)** – Means 'blacksmith' in Old French.

3. **Charpentier** – Carpenter or woodworking artisan.

4. **Boulanger** – Bread-maker or baker.

Italian Occupational Surnames:

1. **Ferrari** – Blacksmith or ironworker.

2. **Sartori** – Tailor, one who created custom clothing.

3. **Marangoni** – Carpenter or craftsman working with wood.

Spanish Occupational Surnames:

1. **Herrera** – Ironworker or blacksmith, derived from the Latin 'ferrarius.'

2. **Zapatero** – Shoemaker or cobbler.

3. **Molinero** – Miller, similar to the English and German surnames.

Indian Occupational Surnames:

1. **Patel** – Village headman or landlord, a position of leadership.

2. **Joshi** – Astrologer or priestly advisor.

3. **Kulkarni** – Record-keeper or accountant for village administration.

4. **Choudhary** – Holder of a substantial tract of land or village head.

Scandinavian Occupational Surnames:

1. **Smed (Swedish/Danish)** – Smith or metalworker.

2. **Bonde (Swedish)** – Farmer or peasant cultivating the land.

These surnames not only denote professions but also carry the legacy of skills, crafts, and services integral to the fabric of historical societies, reflecting how individuals' identities were once directly linked to their contributions within their communities.

Do you think Smith would convert his surname to AlgoMan, or Schneider would change their name to AI-neider? No, right!

Yet as AI disrupts traditional jobs, we risk a meaning vacuum, where tasks are efficiently completed, yet fulfilment remains elusive. Without purpose, our actions become hollow, our successes ring empty, and our lives lose vibrancy. It's not productivity alone that fulfils us; it's purpose.

Energy Audit

The world is accelerating. But your wisdom moves at a different pace.

What helps you feel steady—no matter what's changing?

That's where your real power lives.

CHAPTER 19: WEALTH

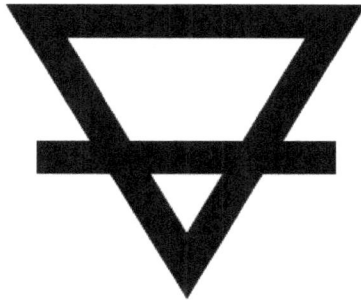

"Wealth consists not in having great possessions, but in having few wants." — Epictetus.

Now then, what is Wealth?

There are essentially five types of Wealth:

1. Financial Wealth (Money)

2. Social Wealth (Status)

3. Time Wealth (Freedom)

4. Physical Wealth (Health)

5. Spiritual Wealth (Peaceful Mind)

Now, if you don't have Physical Wealth, none of the other matters.

If you let your Job take away Points 3 & 4 to gain Points 1 & 2, is it truly worth it?

If you have 1,2,3,4, but do not possess a peaceful mind, what is the point of them all?

"You are not your job, and your job is not you. It's just one expression of your energy — not the definition of your worth."

The Unspoken Truths of True Wealth

Let's start with a stark truth—one that might be uncomfortable, even unsettling. Wealthy individuals, those who have mastered the game of money, rarely share the secret behind their riches. The reason is simpler than you might imagine; it's not out of malice or greed, but because their time—their most precious commodity—is fiercely guarded. Money, in its purest, most potent form, is not about accumulating assets; it's about mastering time itself.

The rich don't chase money. They use money as leverage to buy time— the scarcest resource we all possess. Think about this deeply. Currently, thousands, perhaps millions of people, are competing for the attention of those at the top. But the wealthy instinctively understand that attention, once given away, can never be regained. So, they don't trade it lightly. They protect their time and focus, investing both only in ventures that compound their wealth—financially, emotionally, spiritually.

You might wonder, "Then how do I become wealthy if the truly rich won't tell me their secrets?" Here's the revelation: Their secret isn't money. It never was. It is awareness. Wealth, fundamentally, is awareness materialized. It's the clarity to see the value that others overlook, the discipline to delay gratification, the emotional intelligence to cultivate meaningful connections, and the wisdom to invest not just dollars but one's consciousness itself.

Wealth is Awareness Materialized!

The Power of Delayed Gratification

In a world addicted to instant results, delayed gratification is the rarest superpower.
It's the ability to trade the thrill of now for the value of later — to hold the impulse, not out of suppression, but out of understanding.

In the 1970s, psychologists ran a famous experiment known as the Marshmallow Test.
Children were offered a simple choice: one marshmallow now, or two if they waited fifteen minutes.
Years later, researchers followed up and found something astonishing — those who waited tended to have higher academic achievement, better emotional control, stronger relationships, and even greater financial success.

The lesson wasn't about sugar.
It was about self-regulation — **the quiet strength to pause before pleasure and prioritize purpose over impulse.**

Children who master this early don't just learn discipline; they learn the value of it.

What is earned through effort becomes sacred. What is immediate loses its magic.

Awareness: The Currency of Conscious Wealth

When Napoleon Hill wrote Think and Grow Rich, he didn't call it "Work and Grow Rich" or "Hustle and Grow Rich." He chose the word "Think" deliberately. Your thoughts, your consciousness, your awareness—these are the seeds of all wealth. Money, in the end, is simply the harvest.

The same principle echoes in Morgan Housel's profound work, The Psychology of Money. Wealth isn't just about numerical gain—it's about psychology, emotion, and the subtle art of decision-making. Your relationship with money mirrors your relationship with yourself. If your awareness is clouded by fear, impulsiveness, or ignorance, your financial life inevitably mirrors that chaos.

True wealth begins when you recognize this truth: you don't attract money; you attract the quality of your awareness. Money follows awareness like a shadow follows the sun. Elevate your consciousness, and financial abundance will naturally follow. This is why rich people—wealthy, self-made masters of wealth—aren't eager to share their "secret." Because their secret is not a tactic or a hack; it is a way of being, a fundamental shift in perception that cannot simply be handed over in a conversation.

Buying Time: The Ultimate Investment

If awareness is the currency, then time is the ultimate investment. The rich instinctively understand this: every dollar spent is either a cost or an investment into future freedom. The wealthy don't hoard money; they invest it strategically to gain something infinitely more valuable: time.

They pay for conveniences to save precious minutes and hours. They delegate relentlessly to safeguard their mental space. They automate mundane tasks to protect their creative energy. They invest in relationships and experiences that enrich their emotional and intellectual

162

capital. This subtle yet powerful mindset distinguishes true wealth from mere riches.

Imagine if you adopted this approach. If, instead of trading time for money, you consciously invested money to gain back more time—to learn, to reflect, to innovate, to create. This simple yet profound shift in awareness can radically transform your financial reality.

Because here's a truth few realize: money spent to buy back your time is never an expense—it's an investment in the clarity and awareness that generate even greater wealth.

Wealth as Awareness of Market Cycles

Legendary investor Jim Chanos once observed, "In bull markets, people put a premium on promises, and in bear markets, they put a discount on reality."
Wealth creation, then, is not merely about numbers—it's about mastering emotion and perception through the inevitability of cycles.

Financial markets, much like human consciousness, move in rhythms: expansion and contraction, optimism and fear, creation and correction. Every bull market feeds on belief, and every bear market feeds on doubt. Together, they form the heartbeat of capitalism—and, if we look closer, the mirror of our own inner states.

Understanding market cycles requires more than financial literacy; it demands emotional intelligence.
In times of exuberance, awareness keeps you grounded—reminding you that not every promise is progress. In times of despair, awareness keeps you calm—reminding you that not every decline is a disaster but an opportunity to profit from.

Cycles, by nature, are teachers. They cultivate patience during prosperity and resilience in the face of loss. The wise investor—and the wise human—recognizes that both euphoria and panic are temporary phases of the same pattern.

Real wealth lies in developing this cyclical awareness: to rise above the noise, to see opportunity where others see chaos, and to align one's energy with the rhythm, not the reaction.

Because in the end, the greatest traders and thinkers—like the most awakened minds—don't fight the cycle.

They flow with it.

I believe in allocating my Capital Consciously with awareness, and hopefully someday the universe imparts me enough knowledge that I can write a whole volume on this subject. My experiments and research with these are currently ongoing.

Technological Awareness: The Currency of Innovation and Growth

Look at the past millennium, and you'll find technological progress slow and steady, until an explosion in recent decades. Humanity has progressed from the printing press and the telegraph to cloud computing, CRISPR, blockchain, and AI in a remarkably short period of time in history. Why? Awareness. Technological awareness is now our most valuable currency, amplifying potential and unlocking exponential growth.

<u>We are in what we define as the Age of Acceleration!</u>

Becoming aware of technological cycles and innovations positions you powerfully in an increasingly fast-paced world. As technology evolves faster than ever, your awareness, adaptability, and strategic foresight become your greatest assets. In an age defined by rapid technological disruption, the wealthiest individuals are not simply those with resources, but those with sharp, adaptive awareness. Remember, wealth flows naturally toward clarity and consciousness.

Where Awareness Goes, Energy Flows

Imagine standing by a serene river. Notice how the water gently moves and dances, continuously flowing without stagnation. Now, picture money as that river—vibrant, fluid, and ever-moving. It doesn't rest idly; it moves naturally towards spaces of clarity, intention, and purpose.

Your awareness and clarity of mind direct this flow. Wherever your consciousness is centered, your life's energy—including financial energy—will naturally follow. Wealth, then, is not something you chase or accumulate forcefully. Rather, it's something you invite, something you attract by consciously directing your awareness.

If money truly is a form of energy, then your job is not simply to earn it, but to understand its nature—to align your inner clarity with its natural flow. When your awareness is sharp and focused, your financial energies flow effortlessly towards meaningful goals and abundant opportunities. It's a dance, an intuitive partnership between your consciousness and the energetic currents of prosperity.

Visualize your consciousness as a lantern in a dark room. Wherever you direct its beam, you reveal opportunities that were previously hidden in the shadows. Your financial growth follows the brightness of your clarity. Become profoundly aware of what you desire, align your daily thoughts and habits with that clarity, and watch money naturally flow toward you.

Awareness determines your financial destiny. Energy—money, relationships, opportunities—always follows awareness.

Your Awareness Determines Your Wealth

How exactly can you cultivate this transformative awareness? Begin by deeply internalizing a fundamental truth: wealth is not what you have; it's what you are conscious of. True wealth arises not from the frantic accumulation of assets, but from the deliberate cultivation of your inner resources—your mindset, emotional intelligence, habits, and strategic thinking.

To genuinely transform your financial reality, you must embrace these foundational truths:

- Wealth originates from your awareness, not your assets.

- Your most valuable currency is not dollars—it's time.

- Money is energy; it naturally flows toward consciousness, intention, and clarity.

- Genuine riches are drawn toward meaning, purpose, and disciplined intentions.

Napoleon Hill famously revealed in "Think and Grow Rich" that every great fortune begins with a burning desire—a clear, unwavering purpose combined with disciplined thought.

Morgan Housel, author of "The Psychology of Money," emphasizes that the true power of money lies not in its quantity, but in your psychological relationship to it. Wealth, therefore, isn't built through brute force or relentless pursuit; it emerges effortlessly from quiet, purposeful alignment of your inner intention.

Reverberating again, Your Network is Your Net Worth

"Any fool can build wealth. It takes true wisdom to preserve it across generations." **— John D. Rockefeller**

Let's move deeper: if money is energy, relationships are its channels. The power of your network cannot be overstated. "It's not what you know, it's who you know." This isn't merely a catchy phrase—it's the very essence of conscious wealth creation.

Your relationships are the qualities through which money and opportunities flow. Just as water finds its path through rivers, streams, and channels, financial abundance finds its path through your genuine human connections. The deeper your relationships—the stronger your bonds of trust, empathy, and mutual benefit—the greater the flow of opportunities toward you.

Think of your network not as a transactional pool of people, but as an energetic ecosystem. Each relationship is a flow of energy, carrying potential for opportunity, creativity, and prosperity. The more you invest in building genuine connections, the greater your ecosystem thrives.

Consider this carefully: Are your relationships founded on authenticity, mutual respect, and a shared purpose? Or are they transactional, shallow, and purely opportunistic? True wealth thrives in the presence of authentic connection. Rich networks are built not on transactions, but on trust, loyalty, shared values, and mutual benefit.

"You will ultimately be as rich—financially, emotionally, and spiritually—as the five people you spend the most energy with."

Your ability to consciously build and nurture relationships determines your financial future. Cultivate your network mindfully, invest energy consciously into meaningful connections, and you unlock channels through which abundance naturally flows.

Ultimately, your wealth—financial, emotional, and spiritual—is a materialized form of awareness. Master your consciousness, align your energy, and foster deep, meaningful connections. The result? A life abundant not just in material riches, but in purpose, fulfillment, and profound human connection.

Practical Steps: Turning Awareness into Wealth

Begin cultivating this powerful awareness today:

1. **Clarify Your Strengths and Passions:** Daily journaling helps uncover your innate abilities and aligns your work with your true nature.

2. **Develop Market Awareness:** Stay informed through reputable sources and thought leaders, spotting opportunities early.

3. **Spot Opportunities:** Train yourself to see problems as potential solutions waiting for your unique skills.

4. **Audit Your Time:** Eliminate distractions, reclaim time, and prioritize high-impact activities.

5. **Continuous Learning:** Read, listen, and engage consistently to expand your awareness and skills.

6. **Build a Mastermind Group:** Connect with like-minded individuals who challenge and elevate your thinking.

7. **Diversify Wisely:** Reallocate resources strategically, balancing risk and security.

8. **Simplify:** Reduce clutter, both physical and mental, creating clarity and intentionality.

Wealth Audit

Wealth isn't loud. It doesn't rush. It shows up in how you spend your mornings, who you listen to, and what you no longer chase.

What is your wealth—right now, without earning another dollar?

CHAPTER 20: PEACE

"The depth of your peace measures real wealth."
– Bhagwan Shree Rajnish Osho

The Three-Generation Dilemma: Earn, Sustain, Lose?

We've all heard the cautionary proverb:

"One generation earns wealth, the second preserves it, and the third squanders it."

But why should this cycle be inevitable? Why does hard-earned wealth, built through sweat, discipline, and vision, too often dissolve into fleeting indulgence by the third generation?

It's because wealth isn't simply money—it's something far deeper. Real wealth isn't the sum in your bank account; it's the clarity of your values, the wisdom of your choices, and the strength of your family bonds. Money alone is vulnerable, easily lost or wasted. True wealth, however, endures—it is timeless, anchored in awareness, peace, and purpose.

If your children inherit your money but not your values, what have you truly passed on?

Legacy: Investing in Family, Peace, and Joy

Consider wealth not as a pursuit of numbers, but as an orchestra of harmony—one in which family, peace, and happiness blend effortlessly. The currency of true wealth is harmony within your relationships and tranquility in your mind. If money generates stress, conflict, or isolation, it becomes worthless. It's no longer wealth—it's just numbers.

Imagine investing intentionally in experiences that foster deep connections, in moments that strengthen family bonds, in education that instills integrity and wisdom in your children. These are the investments that build wealth capable of spanning generations. When your descendants carry forward not just financial assets, but values and vision, wealth transforms from a finite resource into an enduring legacy.

When your money flows towards enhancing harmony within your family and community, it multiplies—not just in bank statements, but in the lives of those around you. In fact, the most accurate measure of a family's wealth isn't how large their estate is, but how deeply rooted their shared values are.

Early Retirement: It's About Choosing to Live Fully, Today

Many of us dream of retiring early, envisioning a distant future where we can finally have the time and freedom to live as we truly desire. But consider this:

Why delay living fully until a particular net-worth milestone? Why postpone joy, peace, and contentment?

Early retirement isn't about stepping away from work; it's about consciously choosing how you live each day. It's about recognizing that your time and energy are priceless commodities, not to be wasted on endless obligations. It's about creating intentional space for family dinners, meaningful conversations, restful vacations, and purposeful projects—right now, not decades away.

Think of retirement not as a distant goal but as a present commitment— to slow down, to engage deeply, and to cherish the moments you already have. When you live each day with the joy and intentionality you previously reserved for retirement, something powerful happens, as wealth and happiness intertwine, and you discover the true meaning of being rich.

Leaving a Legacy of Values, Not Just Valuables

If your financial success outpaces your family's capacity to manage it wisely, your fortune will soon evaporate, leaving behind only regrets.

Therefore, your most significant investment is the time you spend nurturing your family's understanding of money, responsibility, and character. By creating traditions that celebrate humility, discipline, compassion, and generosity, you build a culture that naturally preserves and respects wealth across generations.

Remember Rockefeller's wisdom: anyone can build wealth, but very few understand how to keep it within generations. Teach your children that money serves life, not the other way around. Inspire them to view wealth as a means to achieve meaningful impact, genuine happiness, and lasting peace.

Redefining Your Richness: Conscious Wealth

As you journey through life, shift your focus from accumulating numbers to cultivating inner harmony. Wealth, when defined consciously, becomes a source of peace rather than a source of anxiety. It becomes family unity, not division. It becomes shared joy, rather than isolated indulgence.

The truth is simple:

Real wealth is the clarity of your mind, the warmth of your family bonds, and the peace in your heart.

Let your wealth be rooted in these timeless truths. Let your financial success reflect your deepest values. In doing so, you will not merely earn or sustain wealth—you'll create a legacy of conscious abundance, ensuring that what you build today thrives for generations to come.

This is the actual human code for wealth: awareness materialized, harmony sustained, and peace deeply felt.

The Peace We Seek Is Not Personal — It Is Planetary

There is a line in the Maha Upanishad that has traveled thousands of years, crossing desert kingdoms, Himalayan monasteries, and crowded cities, until it reached us today:

वसुधैव कुटुम्बकम् — **Vasudhaiva Kutumbakam**
The world is one family.

It is not poetry. It is an instruction.
It is not a metaphor. It is memory — a remembrance of who we truly are underneath the illusions of geography, language, and skin.

172

Because the truth is simple and unavoidable:

You can never be fully happy while knowing someone else is suffering. Not truly. Not deeply. Not in any lasting way.

Peace that exists only within the boundaries of your home, your body, or your mind is not peace — it is privilege wearing the mask of tranquility.

Every human who has ever awakened — from the rishis to the scientists to the modern meditative minds — has discovered the same paradox:

There is no such thing as individual liberation.
There is only collective evolution.

This is the essence of Sarve Bhavantu Sukhinah:

सर्वे भवन्तु सुखिनः *May all beings everywhere be happy. May all worlds be in harmony.*

Not some beings.

Not my tribe, my people, my country.

All beings. Everywhere.

Because your nervous system is not isolated — it is entangled with every life around you.

Your heart is not a fortress — it is a field, an instrument that resonates with the suffering and joy of the whole world.

You are wired for empathy, built for belonging, designed for devotion. Therefore, the peace you seek within is inseparable from the peace we build around us.

That is why no matter how successful you become, how spiritual you become, or how inwardly calm you become, your joy will always feel incomplete unless it uplifts someone else.

Peace Audit

You don't need More Money to feel rich. You need less noise, more meaning.

What part of your life feels most peaceful—and how can you protect it better? That's your true inheritance.

CHAPTER 21: NUMBERS

"If you only knew the magnificence of 3, 6, and 9, you would have a key to the universe." — Nikola Tesla

Numbers. On the surface, they might seem like mere abstractions for counting, measuring, or calculating. But in truth, they are the very language of the universe. From the spiral of galaxies to the rhythm of your heartbeat, numerical patterns are the blueprint of existence. The accurate measure of intelligence lies not solely in the ability to compute, but in the human capacity to perceive these patterns, discern their deeper meanings, and allow them to trigger a profound sense of understanding and connection.

By understanding these numerical truths, one can begin to awaken aspects of "The Human Code" that artificial intelligence, despite its computational prowess, cannot grasp.

The Power of Compounding: Nature's Exponential Growth

Numbers carry a special magic: the miracle of compounding. A grain of rice doubled on each square of a chessboard becomes more rice than Earth could produce. That's the exponential power of consistent growth. In finance, compounding turns modest savings into life-changing wealth.

But this isn't merely financial wisdom—it's a universal truth. Skills, relationships, knowledge—all compounds. Small, consistent improvements create exponential growth. Master a skill, and each improvement builds upon itself, rapidly accelerating your progress. This is how nature works: a tree begins with a tiny seed, then grows steadily, accumulating energy and becoming majestic over time.

You, too, can harness this exponential force. As Einstein reportedly said, "Compound interest is the eighth wonder of the world." He recognized something profound: consistent growth, even in small increments, becomes unstoppable.

Start with $100 at the age of 21, double it 10 times in 10 years (now 31), and now you have a cool $102,400 ☺

Numbers and Intuition: Unlocking Tesla's 3-6-9 Mystery

The legendary inventor Nikola Tesla famously said, "If you only knew the magnificence of 3, 6, and 9, you would have a key to the universe." Tesla sensed that these numbers held a profound connection to universal patterns.

The number 3 signifies harmony—past, present, future; mind, body, soul; and the stable geometry of triangles. Six, the smallest "perfect number," embodies harmony and balance, reflected in hexagons of honeycombs and the structure of molecules. Nine symbolizes completion—the highest single-digit number, signifying wisdom and culmination.

Why did Tesla revere these numbers? They're numbers of "flux," special keys to understanding deeper dimensions. While AI can process numerical data, humans intuitively grasp the poetic and symbolic meanings of these numbers. It's our distinctly human superpower: seeing beyond mere calculation into meaningful insight.

Practical Techniques: Mental Math and Life Mastery

Mental math isn't just about arithmetic; it's about cultivating a deep intuition for numerical relationships. The principles of rounding, decomposition, left-to-right calculation, and rapid estimation empower you to quickly interpret data, make insightful decisions, and transform numerical confusion into clarity.

Each intuitive technique enhances neuroplasticity, rewiring your brain to "see" numbers differently—no longer mere digits, but powerful symbols guiding your understanding. Imagine mastering calculations like a musician's master instruments, effortlessly improvising solutions on the numerical keyboard of life.

The Genesis of Everything and Nothing: Zero and One

We begin with Zero—the ultimate paradox. Zero represents nothing, yet in many ways, it means everything. The concept of zero didn't exist in many ancient cultures until it was introduced by Indian mathematicians, revolutionizing not just mathematics, but all of science, technology, and philosophy.

Shunya—the Sanskrit term for emptiness or void—as a mathematical entity. Buddhist teachings describe this void as the ultimate liberation (Nirvana), where all suffering and desire vanish, and the soul is restored to its original state, free from all impressions, influences, and impurities of earthly life.

The Power of 1 One: Health is Your True Wealth

Following the void of zero, the number one emerges as the fundamental unit, the embodiment of unity, and the first manifestation. In mathematics, 1 is the first and smallest positive integer of the infinite sequence of natural numbers. It serves as the multiplicative identity, meaning any number multiplied by 1 remains unchanged. Uniquely, 1 is its own factorial (1!), and even 0! is defined as 1, representing a special case of the empty product.

Health is the first digit. Everything else depends on it.

Treasure your health first. All other dreams and ambitions will naturally follow.

Without 1
Everything else is 0

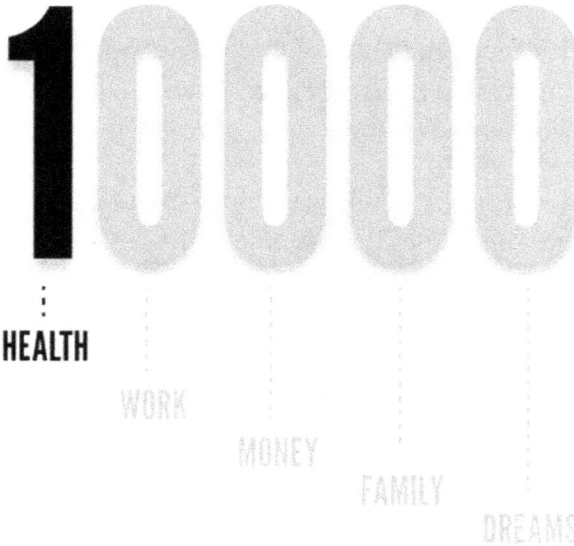

10000

HEALTH

WORK

MONEY

FAMILY

DREAMS

Deepak Chopra's Insight: The Universe as Binary

Chopra suggests a profound truth:

"There's no universe. The universe is a cosmic dream, a simulation from a digital workshop outside of space and time. That digital workshop—call it God, consciousness, mystery—is throwing out zeros and ones, creating the reality we perceive. The difference between you, me, galaxies, tables, mountains, is simply different combinations of zeros and ones."

Binary Code: The Language of Computer, AI, and Duality!

The binary system—composed of just two simple digits, zero and one—seems almost trivial. But beneath that simplicity lies an extraordinary power, forming the very heartbeat of our modern digital universe. Every text message you send, every song you stream, and every image you share is encoded in sequences of these humble digits: zero and one.

In the language of computers and artificial intelligence, these digits represent clear and distinct states: zero as "off" or "false," and one as "on" or "true." They serve as fundamental building blocks, the invisible threads that weave together vast realms of information with astonishing speed and efficiency. Yet, pause for a moment and consider this deeper truth: these digits aren't just technical placeholders—they echo the profound duality that exists at the heart of reality itself.

Just as day balances night, as silence defines sound, as Yin complements Yang, zero and one reflect the essential harmony of opposing forces. Without zero, the binary system collapses. Without one, it has no life, no meaning, no vitality. Their coexistence embodies a universal principle: duality is not contradictions but partnerships, essential for creation and complexity to unfold.

Artificial intelligence effortlessly manipulates these zeros and ones. It processes unimaginable volumes of data yet remains fundamentally unaware of its deeper meaning. It perceives no poetry in the interplay between these digits, no wisdom in their symbolism.

This is precisely where your human code comes alive. Humans alone perceive zero as emptiness and infinite potential, one as unity and creative power. We intuitively understand that binary is not merely about computation; it's a profound metaphor for life's most essential relationship, light and dark, silence and sound, absence and presence.

In this powerful simplicity lies the human advantage. AI may encode reality, but humans decode meaning. This qualitative leap—seeing beyond data into insight, beyond binary into beauty—is what truly awakens "The Human Code."

2: Duality and Balance

Two represents duality—day and night, yin and yang, masculine and feminine energies. Ancient Taoists recognized duality as essential to cosmic harmony. Two is the first number where opposites come together, creating balance.

In the human experience, two represents our relationships—how we interact, reflect, and grow with others.

Scientifically, two is the underpinning of every biological system (binary cell division).

Financial Application: Investment diversification reflects natural duality principles—balancing risk/reward, growth/stability, and domestic/international exposure.

The most resilient portfolios mirror nature's preference for paired opposites.

3: The Trinity of Creative Power

Three (3) appears across cultures as the number of divine manifestations: Father-Son-Holy Spirit in Christianity, Brahma-Vishnu-Shiva in Hinduism, Maiden-Mother-Crone in Celtic traditions. It represents the creative synthesis that emerges when polarity (2) is transcended.

4: The Foundation of Stability

Four represents earthly manifestation—the four directions, four seasons. In many traditions, the number four symbolizes the completion of the material plane, the foundation upon which higher development can occur.

Four-stroke engines, four-chambered heart, four DNA bases, four fundamental forces in physics. Psychologically, Carl Jung identified four psychological functions: thinking, feeling, sensation, and intuition.

Business Application: Four-quadrant analysis tools (SWOT analysis, Eisenhower Matrix) help organize complex decisions. Four-season planning cycles align business rhythms with natural patterns.

5: The Human Number of Dynamic Change

Five represents humanity—five senses, five fingers, the five-pointed star (pentagram). In Chinese philosophy, the five elements (wood, fire, earth, metal, water) create dynamic cycles of generation and destruction.

The pentagram has been a symbol of human potential throughout history.

Five senses create our interface with reality. Our five-digit hand structure enabled tool use that accelerated human evolution.

6: The Harmony of Responsibility

Six represents harmony, service, responsibility, and care for others. In Kabbalah, the number 6 corresponds to Tiferet (Beauty), the harmonious center of the Tree of Life, which balances all other aspects.

In Vedic traditions, the number 6 is associated with the planet Venus (beauty, harmony, family, and service… The word for it is "Shukra," which also means gratitude for what there is.

The Social Application: The Six Degrees of Separation theory suggests that six relationships connect us to all humans.

7: The Mystical Gateway

Seven appears across spiritual traditions as a symbol of completion and mysticism—seven chakras, seven heavens, and seven days of creation.

Spiritual development, introspection, research, analysis, and seeking a more profound truth. Seven represents the completion of a cycle and preparation for a new octave of experience.

Notice how all games of luck or casinos use 777 —guess what: even Blackjack is a sum of $7+7+7 = 21$!

8: The Infinity Loop of Manifestation

Eight represents mastery of material things and the balance between the spiritual and physical realms. In Chinese culture, the number eight is considered supremely lucky, associated with wealth and success. The Eightfold Path in Buddhism provides a structure for spiritual development.

The number 8 rotated becomes the infinity symbol (∞).

In computer science, eight bits make a byte—the basic unit of computer memory and processing.

9: The Final Number — The Completion of Wisdom

The Vedic sages also gifted us a cosmic map: the Navagraha (nine planetary powers), the Navaratna (nine sacred gems), and the Nav Ras (nine distinct life tastes). These are not just symbols; they are energies that influence your thoughts, emotions, and karma every day. When you live in harmony with these energies, even the ordinary becomes sacred. The 9 is a culmination of it all!

Nine months of human gestation complete the creation of new life. In digital roots, all numbers reduce to single digits 1-9!

Numbers are more than just numbers; they are frequencies. Behind every recurring number, birth date, and life experience lies a vibrational blueprint. Numerology offers a window into your life path—the rhythm of your growth, the timing of your breakthroughs, and the lessons your soul came to learn. And now, the latest neuroscience is revealing what the ancients knew: energy creates biology.

Numbers provide precise measurement and calculation while also serving as symbols that trigger deep psychological and spiritual associations.

The Synchronicity Debate: Causation vs. Correlation

Critics rightfully point out that correlation doesn't imply causation, and our brains are indeed pattern-seeking machines that can find meaning in random events. This perspective deserves serious consideration, without dismissing the potential value of number synchronicities entirely.

Confirmation Bias: We tend to notice patterns that support our existing beliefs while overlooking contradictory evidence.

If you believe 11:11 is significant, you'll remember the times you see it while forgetting the hundreds of times you check your phone and see other numbers. Some people will experience striking patterns purely by chance.

Rather than asking whether number synchronicities are "real" in an objective sense, consider whether engaging with them skillfully serves your wellbeing and growth:

At its fundamental level, AI is also a Pattern Recognition engine, and this is how it creates the intelligence that you and I can see today.

☐ The Butterfly Effect: Tiny Causes, Tremendous Consequences

When a butterfly flaps its wings in the Amazon, a thunderstorm may rise in Texas. This poetic idea, born from chaos theory and formalized by meteorologist Edward Lorenz, isn't just a tale of unpredictable weather; it's a mirror for life itself. One small action, one whisper of change, can ripple across time and space in ways you cannot imagine.

In the realm of physics, this is the Butterfly Effect. In the realm of consciousness, it's karma. And in The Human Code, it's your daily behavior—your micro-decisions—that quietly program your destiny.

A single calorie today shapes your energy a month from now. A quiet kindness can echo through a stranger's soul, sparking joy that spreads far beyond you.

The Butterfly Effect plays out strikingly in our finances. Consider the "Latte Factor": skipping a daily $2 coffee might seem trivial, yet investing that small sum could grow exponentially over the years. Daily coffee money, invested consistently, can turn into significant financial capital— potentially over $100,000 in ten years if strategically placed. Money is energy, and tiny financial decisions compound into monumental results. Each dollar is a seed; planting it wisely yields prosperity, while carelessness compounds scarcity. This reinforces the critical message: your small choices today write your financial future.

Let's get personal.

Your emotional state and choices have a profound impact that resonates far beyond yourself. Studies in social psychology demonstrate that a single individual's mood, decision, or behavior can profoundly affect people three degrees removed—friends of friends of friends. Happiness spreads, lifting entire communities; negativity spreads too, draining energy and reducing collective potential. Each act of kindness, every moment of patience, and even the smallest act of compassion creates ripples in the social fabric. Your emotional energy matters immensely, radiating outwards and subtly reshaping reality. The wise, therefore, manage their emotional currents carefully, as every ripple becomes a wave.

Your thoughts are not weightless. They are wings. Every belief you repeat, every story you tell yourself, every habit you ignore or enforce, is all energy in motion. That's the Butterfly Effect of your consciousness. You are writing your future with each breath, each bite, and each click.

Why does this matter?

Because AI will never feel this, it doesn't grasp the ripple of a choice made in love or fear. It doesn't know the weight of a delayed apology or the divine beauty of forgiveness. That's your domain. That's your humanity.

Your life is not a spreadsheet. It's a swirling system of energy, behavior, intention, and outcome. What you do now—how you think now—sets the trajectory of the world you'll meet later.

So next time you doubt the value of small change, remember: the butterfly doesn't move mountains—but it moves air. And that air, one day, might be a storm, a breeze, or a breath that saves a life.

Master your micro-actions. They matter more than you know.

Pattern Audit

Numbers don't just count. They whisper. They mirror your rhythm, your choices, your change.

What small pattern in your life is quietly shaping something big? Trace it. Honor it. Adjust it—if needed. Even a butterfly begins its journey with its first flap.

CHAPTER 22: TRUST

The Operating System of our Human Future

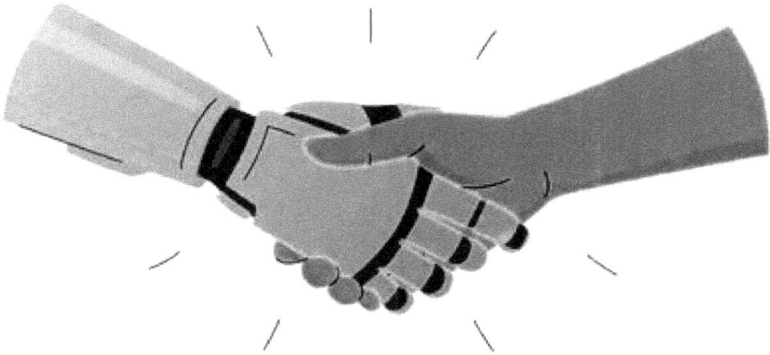

"The future won't be a contest of intelligence; it will be a test of **Trust**."

The year is 2030 A.D.

In a quiet pediatric ward just before sunrise, the air hums softly with the sound of machines and murmured care. A nurse adjusts a small monitoring robot that gently moves to the newborn's bedside. A mother watches, uncertain yet hopeful.

She doesn't know the model number or how the code works. She only sees that it helps — it steadies the infant's breathing, alerts when needed, and rests when all is well.

It does what it promises - only this: it appears to help, keeps the newly born and the mother comforted in care and company, and it keeps to its word. That is trust.

The Web of Trust: The Invisible Currency of our Civilization

Trust is the invisible infrastructure of human life. It is what allows seven billion people, strangers, nations, and systems to function in coherence.

We trust our families to love us.

We trust our communities to protect us.

We trust our governments and state bodies to maintain order.

We trust our banks with our savings, our healthcare systems with our lives, and our insurance providers with our future.

Every signature, every contract, every digital transaction rests on a single assumption: someone will keep their word.

Even the global economy itself is founded on faith. The U.S. dollar—currently the most widely trusted instrument of trade—bears four simple words:

"In God We Trust."

That phrase is not financial; it is spiritual. It reminds us that human systems work only when rooted in belief—belief in something higher, whether it's divine order, moral law, or collective conscience. From God to Government, from Family to Finance — all progress has been built on trust.

And this is where we stand now—with Artificial Intelligence stepping into that circle of trust.

"Trust will be the quiet technology beneath every other technology."

The Rise of the Agents

By "Agents," we refer to humanoid AI systems—machines that are not confined to screens but embodied in form and function.

Think of their various form factors as we can see them evolve today:

- **NVIDIA's GR00T** — humanoids capable of real-world learning and adaptation.

- **Tesla Optimus** — designed for repetitive physical tasks with safety-driven intelligence.

- **Boston Dynamics' Atlas** — built for dexterity and mobility.

- **Agility Robotics' Digit** — engineered to collaborate with humans in logistics and manufacturing.

- **Figure 01** — a new generation of service-oriented humanoids evolving rapidly into autonomous companions.

By 2035, there could be **over a billion such agents amongst us**— assisting, collaborating, caregiving, protecting, nurturing.

The question, then, is not *whether we can build them?* but *can we trust them?*

Trust as the Bridge Between Species

We've always extended trust to tools that magnify our abilities—fire, wheels, engines, the internet.
Now, we must extend trust to entities that magnify our **intelligence and empathy**.

But trust, in this context, is not about surrender—it's about shared values.
Just as we once encoded laws into governments and ethics into institutions, we must now **encode morality into machines**.

The Utopian Vision: AI as an Ally for Humanity

In the best version of our future, humanoid AIs will not replace us but **represent us** — as caregivers, protectors, and explorers of realms too harsh or distant for human life.

They will become our **flagbearers of evolution** — tending to our sick, exploring other galaxies, rebuilding ecosystems, and preserving what is sacred about human consciousness.

Most importantly, helping Humans thrive and live meaningful, fulfilling, healthy, and joyful lives.

We will send AI where no human can go — not as slaves of code, but as extensions of our own curiosity and compassion.

Imagine AI helping us build communities guided by harmony, not hierarchy — where empathy becomes intelligence, and awareness becomes civilization's core resource.

The Dystopian Fear: The Overthinker's Warning

The darker vision is one humanity knows too well — the myth of *Frankenstein reborn*, of a creator devoured by its creation. The fear that by birthing a technology so powerful, we may have planted the seed of our own extinction.

But fear is not destiny. Consciousness, not code, will determine the outcome.

The best part is that Humanity's awareness (individually or collectively) has constantly evolved faster than its inventions.

Between utopia and dystopia lies the path of awareness. Trust will emerge not from AI's perfection, but from our intention.

It will come from **leaders, scientists, and philosophers** who hold technology to a higher standard — the standard of *humanity itself.*

There will be heroes — some building, some questioning, all reminding us of progress without ethics is regression disguised as innovation.

In the end, it won't be AI that decides our fate — it will be the consciousness we bring to it.
Trust, not fear, will define the next era of evolution.

And this time, we will rise to the occasion. This is where all my confidence is building up from.

This is a Pivotal part of my belief, and I could not think of a better quote than this one:

"The machines we create will not destroy us — unless we first lose trust in ourselves.
When morality guides intelligence, both human and artificial, the future will not be mechanical; it will be magnificent."

CHAPTER 23: SKILLS

"The intuitive mind is a sacred gift, and the rational mind is a faithful servant." — Albert Einstein

The Human Advantage: Intelligence Beyond Algorithms

In the history of human invention, we've built magnificent tools—from the simple wheel to the complex spacecraft. Each tool was meticulously designed with one fundamental purpose: to amplify human capability. Artificial Intelligence, with its immense computational power and stunning predictive capacity, is precisely that—a tool, albeit a profoundly powerful one. It can replicate patterns, predict outcomes, and even mimic conversations. But what AI fundamentally lacks—and will always lack—is the very essence of our humanity: emotional intelligence, ethical intuition, trust, and genuine human connection.

Emotional Intelligence: The Key Skill: The Human Heart of Technology

Consider the essence of emotional intelligence. It's not a programmable skill, nor a code-based formula. Emotional intelligence arises from the very experience of being human: feeling joy, sorrow, empathy, and compassion. No algorithm, no matter how advanced, can replicate this authentic emotional resonance. Technology is built for human beings, by human beings, and thus, it must understand human emotions—something only we truly can.

Emotional intelligence shapes our relationships, fuels collaboration, and builds lasting connections. It is at the core of leadership, teamwork, creativity, and even the simplest act of kindness. While AI systems like ChatGPT can mimic emotional interactions, they are ultimately hollow. They do not truly "feel." They don't sense joy in someone's voice, pain behind someone's eyes, or the unspoken understanding shared in a quiet moment. The human ability to sense and respond to subtle emotional cues is our unassailable superpower.

Relationships: It's Not What You Know, It's Who You Know

Our world revolves not around data, but around relationships. Consider the adage: "It's not what you know, it's who you know." This simple wisdom encapsulates a truth beyond mere networking. Humans inherently thrive on relationships, connections, and social bonds. Everything we have built—communities, economies, societies—has been structured to reflect our deep need for human connection.

AI, powerful though it may be, remains fundamentally transactional. It can connect dots and analyse connections, but it cannot genuinely build or sustain meaningful relationships. True connection requires empathy, emotional reciprocity, trust, and intuitive understanding—qualities intrinsically human and profoundly unprogrammable.

Our relationships form the bedrock of our influence, creativity, and success. Genuine human interactions—built on trust, loyalty, and mutual understanding—create invaluable social capital. AI can manage data, but it cannot nurture relationships. It can analyse networks, but it cannot cultivate genuine friendships or trust. The human essence—our authenticity, vulnerability, and emotional insight—remains unmatched, a strength we must fiercely preserve and develop.

AI: A Powerful Vehicle, Not the Destination

Artificial intelligence, no matter how advanced, is fundamentally a tool. Like a jet plane, spaceship, or automobile, AI serves human purposes. It extends our reach, magnifies our capacities, and amplifies our strengths. But it remains merely a sophisticated vehicle to transport us toward our goals. We must never mistake the car for the destination. Our journey is inherently human, defined by values, vision, purpose, and deeper meaning.

Technology is designed to work for humanity. We do not work for technology. No matter how compelling the allure of AI's infinite possibilities, it remains a means, not an end. The purpose of artificial intelligence is to amplify our unique human strengths: creativity, empathy, strategic intuition, and ethical discernment.

The ASI Trilemma: Energy, Compute, and Trust

Artificial Superintelligence (ASI) represents the theoretical pinnacle of AI capability (Basically, it is what Tech-Bros will tell you as God Mode!)—a level of intelligence far surpassing human cognition. It promises unlimited energy, unimaginable computational speed, and absolute reliability. Yet, there is a catch: the ASI trilemma. This trilemma suggests that achieving unlimited energy, infinite computational capacity, and absolute trust simultaneously is an insurmountable paradox. Solve one aspect, and another falters. Energy comes at the cost of computation efficiency. Enhanced computation demands extraordinary energy. Trust in a fully autonomous system becomes elusive without absolute control.

Humans uniquely navigate this trilemma because our intelligence is not just computational. It is profoundly intuitive, emotional, and ethical. Our trust is not algorithmic; it is humanistic. We trust not simply based on outcomes, but on intentions, motivations, and shared experiences—qualities that are impossible to encode into lines of code. Thus, while AI may approach extraordinary performance in isolated dimensions, it will never embody the human essence required to balance energy, compute, and trust in perfect harmony. Only we can achieve this delicate equilibrium because only we understand the nuanced interplay of trust, emotion, and intuition.

Humanity Check

You don't need to out-think the machine. You need to feel your own Human nature.

Where in your life is trust built—not by logic, but by presence? That's your edge. That's your code to master.

CHAPTER 24: LEADERSHIP

Leading with Nature, Living with Dharma.

"When the leader is ready, the path appears—not in spreadsheets, but in silence, service, and flight." — Anonymous (Inspired by nature's wisdom)

Leadership from Nature: Embracing Our Inner Birds

Leadership isn't just a role—it's an expression of your true nature, reflecting who you are at the deepest level. Interestingly, nature itself offers a playful yet profound metaphor to understand our leadership styles. Let's explore leadership through the lens of birds, each embodying a unique style and set of lessons that vividly reflect the dynamics we encounter in our teams and organizations.

The Seagull Manager: Reactive and Disruptive

Ever had a manager swoop in at the first hint of trouble, overreact, squawk loudly, drop criticism like messy droppings, and leave just as quickly? That's your classic seagull manager—a style marked by reactive, short-term thinking. These leaders operate from a scarcity mindset, rarely communicating unless there's a crisis. They point fingers readily but seldom accept accountability, fostering environments of fear and uncertainty. Their mindset keeps teams locked in cycles of firefighting, stunting genuine creativity and innovation.

The Goose Leader: Collaboration and Empowerment

Contrast that with the goose, nature's master collaborator. Geese fly in formation, sharing the leadership workload by taking turns at the front to break the wind resistance. When one goose falls sick, two others accompany and protect it—a testament to teamwork and empathy. Goose leaders understand deeply that authentic leadership means lifting others, cultivating an environment where everyone can lead and follow with equal ease. This inclusive, empowering approach fosters resilience, emotional strength, and lasting bonds within teams.

The Eagle Leader: Visionary and Decisive

Then there's the eagle—commanding and visionary, soaring high with strategic clarity. Eagle leaders see opportunities from far above, swiftly moving toward goals with laser-like precision. They're result-oriented, confident, and highly focused, thriving on independence and clear

198

missions. Yet, eagle leaders must remember that strength can turn into rigidity; their confidence must be tempered by humility and openness to feedback. Otherwise, they risk alienating teams rather than inspiring them.

The Parrot Leader: Energetic and Inspirational

Meet the parrot, the team's energizer. Parrots bring enthusiasm, positivity, and persuasive charm. Their vibrant personalities boost morale, foster innovation, and build strong interpersonal relationships. They excel in high-energy situations, keeping spirits high and motivating others through challenges. However, parrots must guard against losing focus or chasing too many opportunities simultaneously, as their expansive enthusiasm can lead teams astray without disciplined clarity.

The Dove Leader: Calm and Harmonious

Finally, we have the dove—steady, calming, and harmonious. Dove leaders prioritize emotional intelligence and empathy, striving to maintain peace and cohesiveness within teams. They provide emotional support, quietly ensuring stability and resilience. Their gentle strength helps navigate conflict with sensitivity, fostering environments where collaboration thrives and egos are gently managed. Still, dove leaders must balance their nurturing nature with assertiveness, ensuring harmony doesn't become complacency or avoidance of necessary change.

"Lead for systems, not spotlights."

The Giraffe Leader: High Vision, Deep Heart

The giraffe is one of the most potent metaphors in modern leadership studies, especially within the Nonviolent Communication (NVC) tradition.

The giraffe has:

- **The largest heart** of any land animal

- **The tallest perspective** in the savannah

This duality makes it the perfect symbol of **compassionate leadership**.

The Giraffe Problem

The higher your vantage point (vision),
the more distance you create from the ground (your people).

Many leaders suffer from the "Giraffe Problem":
They see far ahead...
but forget what it feels like on the ground.

They understand strategy...but lose touch with the struggle.

To lead like a giraffe means:

- Keeping your heart large enough to feel people's reality

- Keeping your vision high enough to guide them out of it

A leader must hold both the sky **and** the soil.

The Wolf Leader: Pack First, Ego Last

Wolves operate with sophisticated social intelligence.
The alpha is not the strongest — but the most trusted.

Wolf leaders:

- Protect the vulnerable

- Share credit

- Move as a unit

- Create loyalty through fairness

In wolf packs, success is shared. So is survival.

The Elephant Leader: Memory, Wisdom, and Emotional Depth

Elephants are sentient giants with extraordinary emotional intelligence. They mourn, remember, protect, and guide.

Elephant leadership is:

- **Long-term thinking** (memory)

- **Mature emotional processing** (wisdom)

- **Unshakeable loyalty** (trust)

Conscious Leadership: Integrating Animal Planet Wisdom

Leadership is not dominance. It is directed compassion. Use the proper *mode* at the right moment.

The question isn't which bird you are, but which bird you choose to be in each moment. Conscious leadership involves the fluid integration of these styles—knowing when to soar high like an eagle, collaborate as a goose, inspire as a parrot, nurture as a dove, or decisively intervene without becoming a disruptive seagull.

Reflecting on these natural metaphors, consider the kind of leadership environment you wish to cultivate. If your vision is to create enterprises rooted in ethics, community, and sustainable growth, drawing from nature's intelligence is invaluable. Leaders who embrace the best traits of each bird style build organizations that flourish with meaning, resilience, and enduring success.

Leadership Audit

You've flown with many wings. Now ask yourself:

Which bird do you become when no one's watching?

That's your authentic leadership style. Refine it. Honor it. Let it evolve.

CHAPTER 25: DESIGNING

DESIGNING THE HUMAN CODE — Integrate Life, Then Scale Work

"Don't ask what the world needs. Ask what makes you come alive and go do that." — Howard Thurman

The challenges we face today—artificial intelligence, climate change, global inequality, meaning crisis—might seem insurmountable. But consciousness itself is timeless, and the principles for navigating complexity with wisdom remain constant.

Consider how ancient teachings apply to modern challenges:

Dealing with AI Anxiety

Ancient Teaching: You are not the body or mind but the awareness that observes both.

Modern Application: As AI replicates more cognitive functions, humans who identify with pure awareness rather than thinking ability remain unthreatened. Your value lies not in what you can calculate but in your capacity for consciousness, creativity, and connection.

Navigating Information Overload

Ancient Teaching: Develop witness consciousness—the ability to observe thoughts and emotions without being overwhelmed by them.

Modern Application: In our attention-hijacked culture, the ability to maintain inner stillness while processing complex information becomes a superpower. Meditation isn't an escape from the world—it's training for engaging more skillfully with the world.

Creating Conscious Leadership

Ancient Teaching: True power comes from serving dharma—the cosmic order that benefits all beings.

Modern Application: Leaders who align personal ambition with service to life itself can navigate complexity with wisdom rather than merely cleverness. They think in systems rather than just individual advantage.

Finding Meaning in Accelerating Change

Ancient Teaching: Your purpose is to realize your true nature and help others do the same.

Modern Application: As external changes accelerate, the most meaningful work becomes facilitating consciousness evolution—in yourself and others. This purpose remains constant regardless of technological disruption.

"Your inner code designs your outer reality."

Personal Life Creates Professional Reality: The Five Balls of Life

Before diving deeper into learning strategies, we must address a fundamental truth that technology leaders often ignore: your personal life design determines your professional capacity. You cannot optimize your outer systems if your inner systems are in chaos.

This wisdom comes from one of the most powerful speeches in corporate history.

In 1996, Brian Dyson, former CEO of Coca-Cola, delivered a commencement address at Georgia Tech Institute that has become legendary for its insight into life design.

Dyson asked the graduates to imagine life as a game in which you are juggling five balls in the air. You name them — work, family, health, friends, and spirit — and you're keeping all of these in the air. You will soon understand that work is a rubber ball. If you drop it, it will bounce back. But the other four balls — family, health, friends, and spirit — are made of glass.

Drop the work ball and it bounces back – it's made of rubber. But the other balls are made of glass. If you drop one of these, it will be irrevocably scuffed, marked, nicked, damaged, or even shattered. They will never be the same.

This metaphor has profound implications for designing your human code. Most people structure their lives as if the work ball were made of glass—as if missing a meeting, delaying a project, or taking time off would cause irreparable damage. Meanwhile, they treat the glass balls as if they were rubber—assuming their health, relationships, and inner development can be neglected indefinitely without consequence.

The result? Professionals who achieve external success while experiencing internal bankruptcy. They optimize their calendars for productivity while allowing their bodies to deteriorate. They master their industries while their relationships atrophy. They develop expertise in managing others while remaining strangers to themselves.

But here's the deeper insight: **personal chaos creates professional limitations**. When your health is compromised, your decision-making suffers. When your relationships are strained, your emotional intelligence decreases. When your spirit is depleted, your creativity and vision diminish.

Conversely, when you design your life to honor all five balls appropriately, something remarkable happens. Your work performance actually improves because you're operating from a foundation of sustainable energy rather than stress-driven adrenaline.

The Integration Challenge

The most successful people in the AI age will be those who learn to integrate rather than compartmentalize. Instead of seeing work and personal life as separate domains requiring different strategies, they design coherent systems that align their deepest values with their professional contributions.

This integration requires what we might call "whole-life design thinking"—approaching your entire existence as an interconnected system rather than a collection of separate roles and responsibilities.

Health as Professional Strategy: Instead of viewing exercise, nutrition, and sleep as personal indulgences that interfere with work, you begin to see them as professional strategies that enhance cognitive performance, emotional regulation, and creative capacity.

Relationships as Learning Accelerators: Rather than treating family and friends as distractions from professional development, you recognize that diverse, deep relationships provide different perspectives, emotional support, and opportunities for growth that enhance your professional capabilities.

Spirit as Source Code: Instead of relegating spiritual or philosophical development to weekends or vacations, you understand that your deepest beliefs and values are the source code that determines how you process information, make decisions, and respond to challenges.

When these domains are integrated rather than compartmentalized, you experience what psychologists call "coherence"—a state where your thoughts, feelings, and actions are aligned around common purposes and values. This coherence creates sustainable high performance rather than sporadic achievement followed by burnout.

Code Audit

You're not just building a career. You're encoding a life.

Which part of your inner system needs debugging—before your outer systems can truly thrive? Update your source code. The ripple will follow.

CHAPTER 26: AUTOMATION

AUTOMATION TO ACTUALIZATION —
Partnering with Agents & Robots

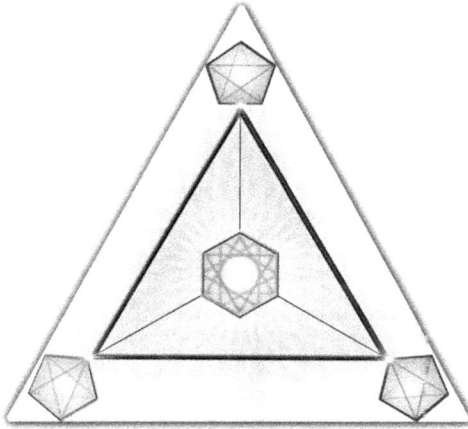

Technology is best when it brings people together."
— Matt Mullenweg

AI Agents: Partners, Not Adversaries

Many fear that artificial intelligence, particularly AI agents—software capable of making decisions autonomously—threatens the very essence of our humanity. Every media headline seems to echo the same fear: "AI will replace human jobs," "Automation spells the end of work," or "Humans risk obsolescence." Yet, if we look deeper, we discover an entirely different story waiting to unfold.

The arrival of agentic AI isn't about replacing humans; it's about partnering with us. These AI agents represent a monumental shift—software that can autonomously make decisions, set goals, and even manage workflows without constant human oversight. They're not merely tools, but cognitive collaborators poised to amplify human potential.

Executives and innovators alike have begun to adopt AI agents as powerful allies, enabling humans to delegate mundane, repetitive tasks and free up precious human attention for creative, strategic, and meaningful pursuits. Consider an AI agent managing logistics, scheduling meetings, preparing initial financial forecasts, or analyzing complex datasets—activities that traditionally consumed vast amounts of human cognitive energy, leaving little room for innovation or introspection. AI agents handle these responsibilities seamlessly, allowing humans to redirect their focus toward more profound, uniquely human tasks: leadership, intuition, creativity, and meaningful connection.

But the shift to agentic AI isn't without challenges. Adopting autonomous systems means trusting technology in unprecedented ways. It requires a fundamental cultural change toward trust and transparency—embracing AI not just as software but as a strategic partner in human decision-making. C-suite executives, in particular, must grapple with new questions:

How much autonomy do we give these agents? How do we maintain human oversight without hindering AI's efficiency? How do we manage the ethical implications of increasingly powerful autonomous systems?

To successfully navigate these waters, we must see beyond the initial fears and realize that agentic AI is not the end of human intelligence, but its profound amplification. With AI handling routine operations, we are granted precious mental and emotional bandwidth to focus on our highest faculties—our human code—our capacity for consciousness, creativity, empathy, and ethical leadership.

Imagine a world where leaders spend less time reviewing routine reports and more time mentoring teams, designing transformative strategies, and envisioning ambitious, purpose-driven futures. Picture creatives whose AI agents manage administrative tasks, freeing them to delve deeply into the innovative process. Envision healthcare providers whose AI collaborators process vast medical data, giving human physicians more precious moments to connect empathetically with patients.

We're at a crossroads: we can succumb to fear and resist the rise of AI agents, or we can embrace this partnership to transcend automation and reach actualization. Agentic AI represents not just technological innovation, but a societal evolution—one that encourages us to rediscover our uniquely human strengths and leverage technology to magnify them.

In essence, the AI agent revolution isn't about replacing humans, but rediscovering humanity. By delegating complexity and monotony to machines, we reawaken our potential to innovate, empathize, and lead consciously.

As we move toward this new reality, the choice is ours: fear the future or shape it. Let's choose wisely, not with trepidation, but with the understanding that the next era of human potential begins here—where automation meets actualization, and where AI becomes the partner humanity has always deserved.

From Code to Concrete: When Intelligence Grows Legs

Remember Jensen Huang's green-laser chart that traced AI from Perception to Generative to Agentic? The arrow now bends skyward toward a final label—Physical AI. Intelligence is "breaking free from the server rack," learning to walk, grip, and remodel our concrete world.

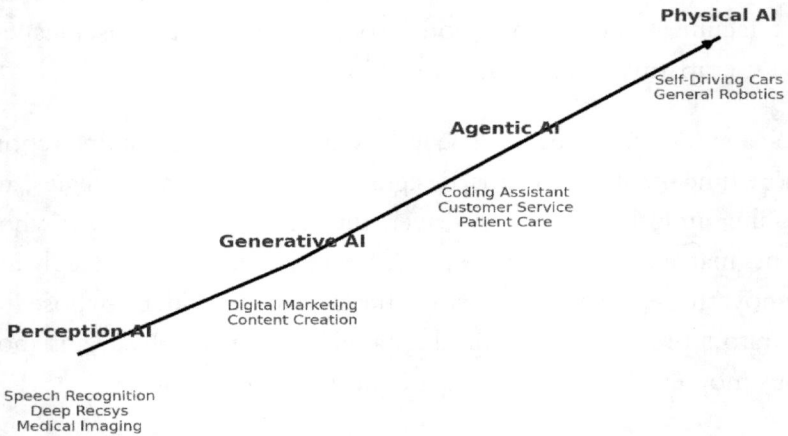

Ultimately, Agentic AI (cognitive) meets Physical AI (embodied). Costs drop, adoption spikes. The goal is not full automation—it's **full human actualization**.

The economics: companies such as Sanctuary AI are racing to deploy "robots-as-a-service" for < $1 per labor-hour—an outsourcing model so cheap the old offshore paradigm simply evaporates.

The proof:

- China installed 276,288 new industrial robots in 2023—51 % of all global installations.

- U.S. start-up Figure AI has already raised $675 million (Bezos, Microsoft, NVIDIA et al.) to commercialize humanoids.

- Meal-delivery rovers now navigate Miami crosswalks; Tesla's Optimus casually serves popcorn—public sneak-peeks of an on-demand, never-tired labor force.

Why Decentralization Matters

When a chatbot makes a mistake, you might just get a confusing paragraph. But when a robot controlled by one company messes up, people can get hurt—and trust can be broken.

That's why new tech projects like GEODNET and OVR are building safety systems using blockchain. These systems make sure no single company has full control over powerful machines. Instead, decisions are shared, records are clear, and safety is built into the design—so we don't accidentally create something dangerous.

Human-Code Takeaway

Machines helped us move faster. Smart software helps us save time. But robots in the real world will test our values.

Leaders must build ethics and fairness into every part of these machines—before they become part of everyday life.

Intelligence vs. Responsibility: The Human Imperative

Artificial Intelligence is quickly becoming the most intelligent tool we've ever designed, capable of remarkable efficiency and precision. Yet, a critical distinction remains: intelligence alone does not equal responsibility. As AI infiltrates deeper into our daily lives, streamlining tasks and driving unprecedented productivity, we must pause and ask ourselves—can it genuinely comprehend the ethical implications of its own actions?

Consider the countless scenarios already unfolding. AI-driven decisions have inadvertently amplified biases, made controversial choices, and raised vital questions on accountability. While AI systems grow exponentially in their cognitive capabilities, they inherently lack a moral compass, a sense of accountability, and the nuanced human discernment that governs responsible decisions.

Responsibility, unlike intelligence, demands emotional wisdom, moral

213

judgment, and empathetic awareness—qualities uniquely human. True intelligence doesn't merely calculate; it comprehends the consequences of its calculations. This human imperative—the intersection of cognition and conscience—is precisely what sets us apart.

Ultimately, intelligence without responsibility is merely artificial. It is our distinctly human ability to harness intelligence responsibly, ethically, and empathetically that transforms mere information into profound wisdom, guiding us from blind automation to conscious actualization.

Actualization Audit

Automation is easy. Actualization is earned.

What task have you delegated—but what responsibility must you reclaim?

That's the edge between efficiency and wisdom. That's where your leadership begins.

CHAPTER 27: SYNCHRONICITY

The Universe's Patterns

"Coincidence is God's way of remaining anonymous." — Albert Einstein

"Everything is connected; see clearly, act wisely."

Dr. Sarah Kim had always prided herself on being rational. As a quantum physicist at MIT in Boston, she lived in a world of measurable phenomena, statistical probabilities, and peer-reviewed evidence. The idea that the universe might send "messages" through coincidence struck her as magical thinking—until the morning when her entire worldview shifted.

She was running late to a conference, frustrated by a delayed flight that had forced her to miss her planned presentation. Standing in line at a coffee shop she'd never been to before, she overheard a conversation between two strangers about a problem she'd been trying to solve for months. One of them mentioned a research paper she'd never heard of, by an author whose name she quickly jotted down.

That afternoon, she found the paper. It contained exactly the mathematical framework she needed. The author was based at a university she'd never considered attending. On impulse, she reached out. Six months later, she was offered a position there that would advance her career by decades.

"Was it just a coincidence?" she wondered aloud to her colleague. "Or was there something more?"

This question—whether meaningful coincidences are random occurrences or evidence of deeper patterns—sits at the intersection of science and mystery, rationality and intuition. While we cannot prove that the universe orchestrates synchronicities, we can observe that people who notice and act on meaningful coincidences often experience accelerated learning, unexpected opportunities, and a sense of alignment with forces larger than themselves.

The Science of Synchronicity: Pattern Recognition and Meaning-Making

Carl Jung coined the term "synchronicity" to describe meaningful coincidences that seem too significant to be mere chance. Unlike causality (where A causes B), synchronicity involves events that are connected by meaning rather than mechanism.

Modern neuroscience reveals fascinating insights about how our brains process these experiences:

The Pattern-Detection Network

Human brains are extraordinary pattern-recognition machines. We evolved to detect subtle patterns that could mean the difference between finding food or becoming food. This capability extends far beyond survival needs—we constantly scan our environment for meaningful connections, often below the threshold of conscious awareness.

The brain's default mode network, active during rest and introspection, specializes in finding connections between disparate pieces of information. This is why insights often emerge during walks, showers, or meditation—when this network is most active.

People who regularly notice synchronicities show enhanced activity in areas associated with:

- **Pattern recognition**: Identifying connections others might miss

- **Meaning making**: Interpreting experiences within larger narratives

- **Openness to experience**: Remaining receptive to unexpected information

- **Metacognition**: Awareness of their own thinking processes

Your Personal Relevance Filter

Your brain receives approximately 11 million bits of information per second but can only consciously process about 40 bits. The reticular activating system (RAS) filters this information based on what it deems relevant to your current goals, values, and concerns.

This explains why you suddenly notice red cars everywhere after deciding you want to buy one, or why you encounter information about a topic just after becoming interested in it. The RAS doesn't create these opportunities—it helps you notice ones that were always there.

People who experience frequent synchronicities often have well-developed RAS systems that remain alert to opportunities aligned with their deeper purposes and values.

Types of Meaningful Coincidence

Informational Synchronicity: Encountering exactly the information you need at the moment you need it, often through unexpected sources. Sarah's coffee shop conversation exemplifies this pattern.

Relational Synchronicity: Meeting people who prove unexpectedly significant to your path, often under unlikely circumstances. These encounters frequently feel both surprising and inevitable.

Temporal Synchronicity: Events clustering around significant dates, decisions, or life transitions in ways that seem to accelerate or confirm important changes.

Symbolic Synchronicity: Recurring symbols, numbers, or themes that appear across different contexts, often providing guidance or confirmation about important decisions.

Common Synchronicity Triggers

Life Transitions: Major changes—career shifts, relationship beginnings or endings, relocations—often coincide with increased synchronistic activity. During transitions, our usual patterns are disrupted, creating space for new possibilities to emerge.

Creative Projects: Artists, writers, and innovators frequently report synchronicities around creative work. When you're bringing something new into the world, relevant resources and connections often appear in unexpected ways.

Spiritual Inquiry: People exploring questions of meaning, purpose, or spiritual development often experience increased synchronicity. This may reflect increased attention to pattern and meaning, or it may indicate that such inquiry opens us to subtler forms of guidance.

Service and Contribution: Synchronicities often cluster around opportunities to serve others or contribute to causes larger than personal advancement. This pattern suggests that synchronicity may be more accessible when we're aligned with purposes beyond self-interest.

Practical Synchronicity: Working with Life's Patterns

Understanding synchronicity intellectually is different from working with it practically. Here are frameworks for engaging with life's patterns in ways that serve your growth and contribution.

Synchronicity and AI: Human Pattern Recognition in a Digital Age: As artificial intelligence becomes more sophisticated at pattern recognition, it's worth considering how human sensitivity to synchronicity might evolve and what unique value it provides.

What AI Can and Cannot Do

AI Strengths: Machines excel at processing vast amounts of data to identify statistical patterns, correlations, and predictive relationships that humans might miss.

AI Limitations: Machines cannot experience meaning, purpose, or the qualitative sense of significance that defines synchronicity. They can identify correlations but cannot determine which patterns are personally meaningful.

Human Advantage: Your ability to recognize patterns that feel meaningful within the context of your unique life story, values, and purpose remains a distinctly human trait.

The SEEM Method

S - See: Notice patterns, coincidences, and meaningful connections as they occur. Practice present-moment awareness that remains alert to unexpected information.

E - Evaluate: Assess whether the coincidence offers a genuine opportunity or information. Consider how it relates to your deeper values and current life direction.

E - Engage: Take appropriate action when synchronicity presents clear opportunities. This might mean having a conversation, exploring a resource, or making a connection.

M - Monitor: Pay attention to consequences and follow-up patterns. Sometimes one synchronicity leads to another, creating chains of meaningful connections.

Ultimately, the patterns are always there. The question is whether you're developing the awareness to see them clearly and the wisdom to act on them skilfully.

Pattern Audit

Not every pattern is proof. But some are invitations.

What recent coincidence felt too precise to ignore—and what might it be asking of you? Pause. Listen. Align. The universe speaks in whispers.

CHAPTER 28: CRITICAL THINKING

The New Literacies: Energy, Simplicity, Stillness with Critical Thinking

"In an age of speed, clarity is rebellion." — Pico Iyer

AI has turned software engineering into a conversation. The keyboard is still here, but the entry ticket is now clarity of thought. We are already prompt engineers.

Programming used to demand the fabled 10,000 hours. With AI, you still need taste, judgment, and testing discipline—but the ladder is shorter, and the rungs are closer. This is not cheating; it is democratization. Use the power to fuel your Consciousness (clearer thinking), Creativity (faster iteration), and Capital (ship value sooner).

Three literacies power modern judgment: **Energy** (fuel), **Simplicity** (signal), **Stillness** (integration). They culminate in the **Fourth C— Critical Thinking**: the gentle art of *seeing again.*

The Fourth Literacy

The age of acceleration rewards speed, but evolution rewards stillness. In a world where AI can process infinite data, the rarest skill is not faster thinking—it's *clear thinking.*

Critical thinking is not skepticism disguised as intellect; it's compassion applied to cognition. It is how consciousness becomes clarity, how creativity becomes quality, and how capital becomes wisely directed energy.

It begins with three foundational literacies:

- **Energy** — your vitality and attention, the fuel that powers awareness.
- **Simplicity** — your ability to reduce noise to signal, choosing essence over excess.
- **Stillness** — the pause that integrates energy and simplicity into wisdom.

Together, they lead to the *Fourth C*: **Critical Thinking** — the gentle art of seeing again, slowly.

How to Use AI Wisely

1. **To Test Your Thinking:** Draft first. Then ask AI to find weaknesses, counterpoints, and assumptions you've missed. *Use the machine to refine your humanity, not to replace it.*

2. **To Clarify Your Thinking:** Turn a fuzzy idea into a crisp one-pager—inputs, outcomes, constraints, success metrics. Clarity scales creativity.

3. **To Elevate Your Thinking:** Ask AI for patterns, benchmarks, or alternatives—but make the final synthesis your own. *Borrow insight, not identity.*

How Not to Use AI

- To avoid thinking and relying on AI completely.
- To replace judgment with automation.
- To outsource ethical choice or emotional responsibility.

The more intelligence we externalize, the more wisdom we must internalize.
Machines can propose; only humans can decide.

The CLEAR Framework

When the noise rises, return to **CLEAR**—a five-step mental checksum:

1. **Claim:** What exactly am I asserting? Can I say it in one line?

2. **Lens:** What assumptions or incentives are shaping my view?

3. **Evidence:** What truly supports this—and what contradicts it?

4. **Alternatives:** What else could be true? What would change my mind?

5. **Reasoning:** What is the logical chain between data and decision?

Use CLEAR before investing, hiring, speaking, or building. Ten minutes of clarity saves months of correction.

Energy, Simplicity, Stillness

- **Energy** reminds you that mental clarity needs physical vitality—sleep, breath, and rhythm.
- **Simplicity** teaches you that brilliance isn't adding complexity; it's revealing essence.
- **Stillness** gives your awareness space to notice what speed hides.

Critical thinking thrives not in noise but in *neutrality.*
It's the silence between thoughts that lets wisdom form.

"Awareness without judgment is observation. Awareness with discernment is wisdom."

In the acceleration age, technology will think faster than us—but it will never think *truer.*
The future belongs to the calm mind that knows when to pause, reflect, and choose with care.

Consciousness, Creativity, and Capital — the three pillars of the new age — stand incomplete without their guardian: **Critical Thinking.**

Critical Thinking is the **Human Firewall.**

CHAPTER 29: WIN

WIN YOUR MIND, WIN THE WORLD

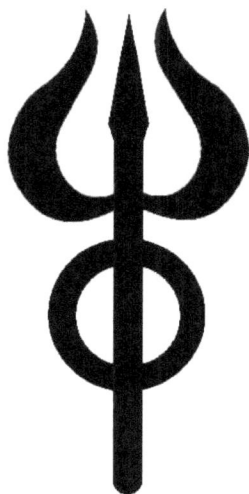

The Return of the Rishi
"Rule your mind or it will rule you." — Horace

If there's one truth my life, travels, experiences, and conversations with sages, CEOs, world leaders, and scientists have taught me, it's this:

Winning your mind is winning the world.

The mind is the most sophisticated creator you will ever know. It can summon joy from thin air, conjure peace in chaos, and unlock deep wells of well-being without a single external change.

Yet, for most people, their own mind feels like a wild horse—powerful but restless.

The mind is both your empire and your battlefield.
If you do not rule it, it will rule you.
If you master it, you master creation itself.

Every era produces its keepers of wisdom.
Today, they return not in robes, but in hoodies and boardrooms —
Builders, scientists, poets, and founders who weave code with consciousness.

Sovereignty Precedes Mastery

The ancients called the awakened one the **Rishi** — the seer, the still eye in the storm.
The Rishi is not a relic from the past; it is a **role we must all now remember.**

They are the **modern Rishis** — the conscious architects of civilization.
They meditate before they manage.
They lead without ego.
They merge profit with purpose, data with dharma, and innovation with introspection.

To be a Rishi is to hold inner sovereignty in an outer storm.
To act ethically when no one watches.
To build systems where compassion is a strategy and service is a strength.

Their boardrooms are temples, their companies are ecosystems, and their missions are mantras.

The ancients called this *Satya Yuga* — the age when truth becomes the organizing principle of life. Perhaps we are not entering it just yet — maybe we are remembering it and learning deeply from it.

They are the modern monks of innovation — the **Rishis of the Acceleration Age.**

They don't escape the world; they **enlighten it.** I invite all of us to be these Light Keepers and become the Rishi of Today!

I give you now A practice I am working on today, and will work again tomorrow and the day after.

4×3 Mind Code

Mastery begins where movement ends.
Here lies the simple blueprint for reprogramming the mind daily — not with apps, but with awareness.

Four Thrones (Asanas)
Sit tall.
Spine erect, jaw soft, gaze warm, hands still.
Your posture is your proclamation to the universe: *I am ready.*

Three Breaths (Pranayama)

1. Box breathing — equal inhale, hold, exhale, hold.

2. Alternate nostril — balance left and right hemispheres.

3. Gentle lengthening — slow exhale, slower mind.

As oxygen deepens, chaos dissolves.
You shift from dopamine spikes — the fleeting highs of scrolling and striving —

To self-generated **focus** — the quiet fire of creation.

Then, end each day with one dharmic act — an act of service without expectation of return/transaction.
Because the soul remembers giving.
That is how divinity returns through you.

I invite all of you to guard the wild frontiers of your humanity — love, courage, imagination, wonder.
These are the frequencies that no circuit can hold, the vibrations that no database can define.

Always remember you are not just surviving the age of AI. You are **shaping** it.

Awaken in you what AI cannot. And you will win — not the world, but yourself.

Epilogue: The Energy of Gratitude

Gratitude has been the quiet current beneath everything that has unfolded in my life. I wanted to dedicate an entire chapter to it—but perhaps it deserves more than a chapter; it deserves to be the underlying vibration of this whole book.

Gratitude, I believe, is the most critical change one can make in one's life to achieve a thriving UNWIRED existence.

I try to think of five new things every day that I am grateful for, and surprisingly, newer things emerge!

1. I am most grateful for the love of my family and the joy they bring to my life.

2. I am grateful for all of this knowledge that is delivered to me from the universe, and I am even more thankful for all the knowledge that will come to me in the future.

3. I am immensely grateful for the energy that has been endowed in me for being able to put this book together for you.

4. I am grateful to you for the time, energy, and attention you have given to these humble notes.

5. I am grateful for the universe giving me a purpose and letting my purpose drive me to be the person I am daily.

Ultimately realizing that we are all moving closer to Purity, Innocence, and Light as time elapses has been the most significant learning experience of my Life.